Dear Susie,

This cookbook be your copy of that cookbook I previously mentioned and own. Many of the recipes and pictures remind me of your mother — I miss her!

Love,

Garrett

7/10/18

Salicyl Obst marmeladen u. Kirsche

Wasser 30 M. Zucker u. 1 Spitze Salicyl. Eine Viertelstunde sieden lassen (Wasser ... Obst ... werden mit ... Salicyl ... gespült werden.

Chocoladesauce zu ...

Chocolade erweichen ... Milch auf ... 2 Dotter einrühren u. nach Geschmack zuckern.

Café Crème

7 M. Zucker 5 Esslöffel ... u. 2 Dotter am ... zu einer Crème schlagen ... 1/4 l. geschlag... Obers dazu.

Gebackene Crème

Vanillecrème wird wie bei Schliefkrapferln in Butterteig gefüllt, ausgeradelt, gebacken, u. Zucker bestreu... u. mit der Schaufel gebraunt.

Salse od. Gelee

Auf 1 Kg. Früchte 1/2 Kg. Zucker Zucker mit entk... Früchte über Nacht stehn lassen. Den nächsten Tag vom Siedepunkt 15–20 Minuten kochen lassen. Nie mehr als 1–1 1/2 Kg. auf einmal machen.

Tante Hertha's

Viennese Kitchen

Tante Hertha's

Viennese Kitchen

A BOOK OF FAMILY
RECIPES

Monica Meehan and Maria von Baich

NEW
HOLLAND

For Hertha and Lene
To the timeless bond of cousins

First published in the UK in 2011 by
New Holland Publishers (UK) Ltd
London   Cape Town   Sydney   Auckland

Garfield House, 86–88 Edgware Road
London W2 2EA
United Kingdom
www.newhollandpublishers.com

80 McKenzie Street
Cape Town 8001
South Africa

Unit 1, 66 Gibbes Street
Chatswood, NSW 2067
Australia

218 Lake Road
Northcote, Auckland
New Zealand

ISBN 978 1 84773 726 7

Publisher: Clare Sayer
Production: Laurence Poos
Design: Jacqui Caulton
Food Photography: Tara Fisher
Food Stylist: Annie Rigg
Prop Stylist: Roisin Nield
Location Photography: Jon Meade
Additional Location Photography: Georg von Baich
All historical photographs were accessed from the authors' family's private collection.

1 3 5 7 9 10 8 6 4 2

Reproduction by Pica Digital PTE LTD, Singapore
Printed and bound in China by C & C Offset Printing Co., Ltd

Contents

Introduction

A Viennese Life

How did *Tante Hertha's Viennese Kitchen* come to be? Why Viennese dishes and who was Tante Hertha?

Tante Hertha's story will come. In some subtle respects, the paths that both my mother Maria and I have taken parallel Hertha's, in the uncanny ways a family's history can find common ground decades later. For many years, a faded brown notebook filled with Hertha's beautifully penned collection of Viennese specialities, entries as early as the turn of the twentieth century, written in peaceful as well as troubled times, lay dormant in a kitchen drawer, quietly waiting to be opened again. These recipes have taken their own physical journey across oceans and back again to make their way into this cookbook as an ode to Hertha's Vienna.

To begin, Tante Hertha had not been one of the mythical figures of my childhood. She was to me part of the interesting collection of names about which my beloved Austrian grandmother and her contemporaries that made up a large circle of extended family and friends, spoke warmly: Tante Vera, Onkel Kurt, Otto Mayr, Tante Olga, Duschan, Onkel Anton, Onkel Bruno, Tante Elsa. They were all *Tanten* and *Onkel*, aunts and uncles, for whom I felt no distinct connection apart from what I imagined the holders of these glamorous names and colourful lives represented in the Vienna of their past, from the early 20th century until the end of the 1960s when Vienna was to change for good.

The day our cookbook was contracted, I called my mother's brother Paul and his wife Marie in British Columbia, Canada to tell them about our project. In her charming, soft French-Canadian lilt, my aunt Marie said 'this is probably nothing for the book, but I remember the day your grandmother was with us in Montreal in the spring of 1971. She came running into the room filled with tears, clutching a letter from home: '*Tante Hertha*

ist gestorben, Tante Hertha ist gestorben!'
pronouncing with such heartfelt sorrow that
Tante Hertha had died. Warm but equally
Victorian, my grandmother was not one to
express emotion in such a way. The loss she
felt, in the sad words the letter would have
conveyed, was the beginning of a door slowly
closing on the Vienna of the past. Almost
forty years later, I began to discover who
Hertha may have really been, beyond just
another beautiful and faded name.

Baroness Hertha Freiin von Winkler was
born in Krain (Slovenia today) on the 2nd
of July 1889 at her family home, the Villa
Samassa, but lived for most of her life in
Vienna. Her father was Baron Egon von
Winkler, a high-ranking official in the
Austrian Ministry of the Interior, and her
mother Bertha (née Samassa) part of a wealthy and illustrious family who
manufactured church bells and candelabra, with orders as far-reaching as South
America. Hertha was my grandmother Helene Galle's first cousin; their mothers were
sisters. Although Hertha was over a decade older than my grandmother, the two
youthful and lively cousins were very close. As young women, they would meet
faithfully every winter in Vienna to attend the annual ball season. The house balls, by
exclusive invitation, were a vital part of every young society woman's calendar.

In the summers throughout the 1920s and early 1930s, Hertha would in turn leave
Vienna for long stays at my grandmother's country estate in modern day Slovenia. At
the end of the First World War, Vienna had witnessed the collapse of the monarchy and
crippling unemployment. Food supply was dismal and there has been severe *Hungersnot*
(food shortages) in post-war Austria, particularly in the cities. Whenever she could get
away from Vienna, Hertha took the opportunity to escape to the countryside, where
prosperity was, for the time being, unwavering.

My grandmother's estate was based in the small hamlet of Freudenthal, meaning
Joyful Valley, bordering the southwestern region of the Ljubljana Marshes, Slovenia.
Originally a monastery, Schloss Freudenthal was a 6,000 square metre building and
spanned 100 hectares of land with vast forests and game for hunting. It was originally
the home of Carthusian monks, built by the Carinthian Duke Bernhard of Spannheim

Left: Tante Hertha, circa early 1920s.
Right: My grandmother, Helene (centre), with her siblings (from left) Onkel Bruno, Tante Christl, Onkel Gert.
Below: My grandfather's brother, Onkel Duschan (driving), his sister Tante Vera, my grandfather Georges behind with his sister, Tante Olga.
Overleaf: Left-hand page: Hertha's birthplace, the Villa Samassa; Right-hand page: Schloss Freudenthal, my grandmother's family estate. Clockwise: The interior of Freudenthal; my mother, Maria as a little girl at the house; my grandmother; the view from the approach to the house; the salon.

in 1255. In the 17th century, it housed a monks' school and a library, which kept numerous valuable manuscripts. In the family since 1836, it was bequeathed to my great grandfather Franz Galle in 1862. The family home in which my grandmother and her four siblings grew up, together with its large staff who ran the grounds, the forestry business, the game farm and the household, replaced the sombreness of the one-time convent with a much more secular vitality. A small chapel however remained intact if infrequently visited.

Far from idle and yet privileged by a charmed life, the two cousins would go horseback riding, play the piano, needlepoint in the garden, read and enjoy the lively banter of generations of family and friends. Space was plentiful and many guests would find their way to the 'joyful valley' each summer to visit the Galle family.

My uncle Paul recalled with affection:

'My memories of Tante Hertha go back to the summers we spent in Freudenthal in the mid- to late 1930s right up to the beginning of Second World War. As a niece of Grandmother Elsa Galle, Hertha had strong ties to Freudenthal – so she frequently left Vienna to stay often for weeks at a time. Offering hospitality at a time of moderately paid servants was not much of a problem. I remember her as a very cheerful presence, who loved fun and jokes (which we kids of course didn't get), and enjoying long walks in the fields or forest. Hertha loved visitors, guests and most certainly good food, even if it was prepared by peasant kitchen maids and not up to Viennese society standards.'

During the First World War, Hertha was a nurse in a military hospital for the Red Cross. It was hardly a career path but an honourable contribution nonetheless to help in the war effort along with so many other young women. After the war, Hertha, who would have been supported by her mother's modest post-war pension, was eager to consider a job opportunity. There were very few suitable prospects for young ladies, and for someone of

Above: My grandmother, Helene, taken by Hertha. On the bottom right of the image you can just make out Hertha's distinctive embossed signature.

Above right: My grandfather, Georges.

Right: My grandparents' wedding at Schloss Freudenthal.

her social standing, even less so. By chance, one of the new professional possibilities open to women was portrait photography, quickly becoming quite the rage in the 1920s. The training would have been rather basic, but Hertha soon acquired darkroom staff and eventually opened a small atelier on the Graben, one of Vienna's most exclusive and fashionable streets in the first quarter of the city. Her notable *Hertha*, embossed on lower right hand corner of the heavy photographic placards alongside the studio's address, was an elegant mark of distinction for the intrepid new photographer.

In 1929, my grandparents married at Schloss Freudenthal. The wedding was a formal yet intimate affair with 27 guests gathering together to celebrate the marriage of Helene Galle and Georges von Baich. Helene's beloved cousin Baroness Hertha of course attended. She had photographed the engagement photo earlier in the year in Vienna and now, the gathering itself. It is a photograph I always remember; my great-grandfather with long white beard and

Above: Hertha's invitation to my grandparents' wedding in April 1929. The front shows the engagement portrait, taken by Hertha. The signatures of all the guests are on the back.
Right: Schloss Freudenthal.

dark suit, beautiful women in 1920s flapper fashion, men in top hats and finally Hertha, sitting at the very edge of the photograph, the image a little too faded to see her entirely. The names again – Vera, Olga, Elsa – captured in the still of Hertha's timeless photograph.

The newly married couple had been presented as a wedding gift a house in Laibach (Ljubljana) to start their family, where my mother was born, before moving on to Marburg and ultimately taking refuge with relatives in neighbouring Austria. Franz Galle passed away a few years after the wedding. His eldest son Bruno would inherit the entire seat and continue to run Freudenthal, which had only just narrowly survived the 1930s stock market crash. By 1944, Germanic families, in particular wealthy landowners, were forced to leave the Yugoslav state or face a communist regime and a critical fate. Overtaken by state militia with great force and speed in a single night, Bruno and his family were stripped of their home with only a few small possessions between them.

Freudenthal was gone. Its long idle summers remained the sharpest of memories for its one-time inhabitants. By 1951, the estate became and remains home to the government-run Technical Museum of Slovenia. Their website states: 'The museum is divided into forestry, woodworking, fishing,

hunting, electrical, agricultural, textile, printing and transport departments. Take part in Saturday workshops and Sunday demonstrations of old machinery and techniques and the use of tools that were used by our ancestors.'

Hertha's photographic studio in Vienna eventually moved from the first to the fourth quarter, still central but no longer *the* address. By the beginning of the Second World War with many more *Foto Salons* (studios) competing for business, the novelty was gone and the ability to maintain an income-generating business slowly fading away.

Hertha remained unmarried and as she and her widowed mother were in need of reasonable accommodation in hard times, they were, as luck (and status) would have it, resituated in the heart of the city. Hertha's brother-in-law Baron Dr. Otto Mayr was a partner of a successful law firm with offices on the ground floor of a building that featured a relatively small but charming living space on the penthouse floor.

Rotenturmstraße 13. There could not have been a better address in Vienna. Set in the very centre of the *Ersten Bezirk*, the first quarter, it was still then a Vienna of wealth and nobility, the elite who had all the right contacts to maintain such central address. Just around the corner sits Vienna's largest cathedral, the 14th-century Stephansdom. Today the area is filled with tourists and ubiquitous chain shops. The neighbourhood of the 1920s through to the 1950s would have been one of elegant austerity and a purposeful air with neighbouring streets of the Graben, the Kärnterstrasse and the Kohlmarkt notably the most fashionable pedestrian streets in the city. These were the streets of Imperial Vienna, its inner core landmarked by a vast palace, the Hofburg.

The apartment became affectionately nicknamed *Die Gipfelhütte*, the 'summit mountain hut', reachable by the unmistakable creaking and clanking and gentle swaying of an old-fashioned lift with decorative iron and glass doors. In order to secure this wonderfully central apartment within the family, Hertha and her mother officially 'adopted' my grandmother's sister, again with the help of the her brother-in-law just a lift ride away. The beautiful and equally intimidating Tante Christl Galle became Christine Baronin von Winkler, and joined Hertha and her mother at the *Gipfelhütte*. When Hertha's mother passed away, Christl's mother (my great-grandmother) joined her daughter and niece and the three ladies continued to bring a lively mix of friends and family through its doors.

My mother's Vienna was different from that of her siblings Theodor and Paul and certainly from Hertha's, who was a true *Wienerin* – citizen of Vienna. From their adopted home town of Graz, my mother and her two brothers were all at some point students in Vienna, overlapping for a relatively short period in the mid 1950s. Limited means made frequent trips home to the Styrian capital prohibitive and with the two dashing brothers much more preoccupied with the social scene than with the concerns of their little sister, the student years could be lonely at times. Invitations from Hertha would come on occasion but most young students would prefer to spend time with friends rather than two elderly aunts and a grandmother, no matter how engaging. Regardless, in the quiet Sundays, something would always draw my mother to Hertha's graceful neighbourhood. There was always life at Hertha's, and just getting within close proximity to the *Gipfelhütte* brought a sense of peace and comfort.

Life at Hertha's meant a sophisticated mix of friends, food, and of utmost importance, the opera. Hertha had a lifelong subscription to the stately Vienna Opera House and was a massive Wagner fan. In the late 1950s, by then approaching her seventies, she thought nothing of sitting for hours and hours (and consecutive days) through *Der Ring der Nibelungen* in its entirety, *Meistersinger*, *Lohengrin* and *Parsifal* and saving each and every program, collecting the autographs of her favourite opera singers. She would discuss the performance at length afterwards with occasional critical judgements concerning individual artists. Tante Hertha always had strong opinions, outspoken and determined and with an air of finality in her comments. Her own family were highly musical and Hertha's family library of sheet music were all impressively noted as pieces for four hands. Her father Egon had friends who had played with Schubert; her Uncle Otto had in the meantime become president of the *Musikverein*, the headquarters for the Society of the Friends of Music and home of the Vienna Philharmonic. He became known as the Music Baron among the city's distinguished musical elite.

A life without music was as unimaginable as her other passion: food and cooking. Sometime after the Second World War when Austria was rebuilding, Hertha decided to transpose her passion into a small catering business for family and friends. With her many contacts and cherished recipes, she was always in demand. The income generated afforded Hertha her many travels, often escorted tours throughout Europe to Spain, Portugal, Greece and Turkey and as far reaching as Morocco.

Hertha's *Gipfelhütte* kitchen was a mansard-style room which in reality was a bathroom with a full size tub, covered with a table top when not in use and above, an on-demand gas-flame hot water dispenser. It was usually very hot in her 'kitchen' and my mother and her brothers can still envision Tante Hertha hunched over a small kitchen table while preparing jams, marmalades and any *Mehlspeisen* she'd concoct on order for her clientele. The waft of Seville oranges in winter to prepare her Orange Marmalade and the smell of sugar, chocolate, raisins and nuts used to make wonderful cakes and biscuits resonated throughout the flat. Whether entertaining or behind the scenes, Hertha's signature large sparkling diamond earrings and equally sparkling bright blue eyes illuminated whichever room she was in.

Despite her liveliness, her regimen was strict. When guests were invited to lunch – never dinner as is customary today – they were immediately seated to an impeccably laid table and were not permitted to leave their seats until the meal was over. Even the youngest of guests could not help clear the table. Hertha was always in charge, every detail perfect.

Uncle Paul, himself a professional landscape photographer who studied graphic design at the prestigious *Graphische Lehr – und Versuchsanstalt* in Vienna, has a recollection from when he was a young boy of nine or ten. It seems to encapsulate the essence of who Hertha was: a modern, independent woman, single, unafraid, adventurous, glamorous, original.

'In the summer 1943 or 1944 Hertha came for a visit to Marburg/Drau (Maribor/Slovenia today), where we lived at the time. She wore a three-quarter length light-coloured silk dress, took me for a walk through town, and was apparently happy to have a male companion escorting her, for, being a hot afternoon, she felt like going into a pub for a beer! Since I had never seen an elegant, white-haired lady with prominent diamond earrings enjoying a beer in a place crammed with teamsters and other working class people, I remember the picture vividly.'

My mother is the true cook in this cookbook. As a schoolgirl, she had spent the beginning of her school years at the Sacré-Coeur in Graz, a Catholic private girls' convent school. For the remaining four years of high school, my grandmother felt it would be

Hertha's cousin, my grandmother, Helene Galle, circa 1918–1920.

beneficial to round out her education in a school that while academic enough to provide a diploma towards entering higher education, focused its curriculum on running a household which, of course, meant learning how to cook. Located on a small square on the *Entenplatz* (Duck Place), the 'duck school' was a kind of finishing school filled with clichés of city girls quick to snicker at a teacher's provincial accent or pedestrian style as young teenaged girls with a naïve snobbishness were likely to do. The students would gather in groups of three once a week to plan a menu and prepare the dishes of the day, starting with a light entrée and eventually graduating to a more intricate selection by the end of term. My mother deeply resented being enrolled in a school referred to in jest as the *Kochlöffel Akademie* – the Cooking Spoon Academy. She said laughingly that her 'cooking spoon' education entitled her to co-author this book.

Growing up, I didn't spend hours in the kitchen at home with my mother licking the icing off a cooking spoon (an Austrian mother would never allow such wastefulness) or learning how to make classic tortes and strudels. In the year spent writing the book, these missing hours in the kitchen were made up over a stove and a laptop learning about the nuances of Viennese cooking by watching, assisting and typing in the savoured ingredients and intricate methods dictated by my mother. My favourite recipe had always been *Tante Hertha's Geburtstagstorte*, not realizing the significance the recipe would hold. I had lived with my grandmother for a year as a university student and the lifelong friends I made remember the special birthday cake too. Hertha's recipes had no true how-to instructions as the methodology was assumed, no measurements of a cake pan or speed setting of an electric mixer and certainly no oven temperatures! Once again, my mother's earlier training and natural culinary talent enabled her to interpret and not simply transcribe these dishes.

In 1959, at the age of 22, my independently-minded mother travelled to Canada by ship, with the intention of staying one year to gain foreign work experience in her chosen profession. She returned to Austria at the end of her year abroad with the ultimate realization that it was to say goodbye to her home country and start a new life in Hamilton, Ontario. As always, she curtsied to her grandmother and hand-kissed Hertha, bidding them adieu one final time.

My mother has never lost her Austrian heritage: her precision for detail, her love of music, her experiences from the Cooking Spoon Academy on Duck Place, and her recollections of her short but impactful time in Vienna.

Hertha had added recipes to the old brown hard-covered notebook throughout her adult life. The actual recipe book still exists, featuring several different handwritings, likely a few entries from Hertha's mother, Hertha herself and possibly those of another aunt or grandmother. A few forgotten receipts and postcards were left gently dotted throughout its pages. When my own grandmother died in 1992, my aunt Ina asked my mother if she would look through a box of old papers and notes that she wasn't intending on keeping. In it, was the slightly yellowed recipe book, still intact despite being abandonned for some time. My mother remembered it from many years ago, kept in my grandmother's kitchen drawer and used only for special occasions as an ode to Tante Hertha and her esteemed Viennese style.

A small but invaluable treasure, my mother was delighted to inherit the journal and bring it back home to Toronto that year. Four years ago, when I purchased a small flat in London, my mother brought the book to me as a housewarming gift.

I was too young to have met Tante Hertha. I was however a guest of the Rotenturmstraße on my trips to Vienna. As a young girl, I remember having to courtesy to the revered Tante Christl. I recall the iron clad lift and the smells of a gas cooker and incredible scent of the freshly made Austrian *Kipferl* from the corner bakery of my grandmother's flat in Graz, and the colourful pink and gold packages of hazelnut wafers packed in my grandmother's suitcase when she came to Canada to visit for the summers. And the handwritten letters on light blue airmail paper, tissue paper-thin and covered with a fine ink pen and distinct European handwriting.

As I walk through my own neighbourhood in London, past stately Georgian homes and Victorian mansion blocks, I think how surreal it feels to be living in the UK (where my father was born), at the edge of the divide between the past and the present, remembering these Austrian moments so vividly. We have immensely enjoyed our very personal project to retrace Hertha's path and as a result, to rediscover mine and my mother's, each of us with overlapping geographies but very different experiences and timelines. As always, the culture of food unites us and the family and friends with whom we share it, binds us.

Tante Hertha, circa 1940.

Background

A VIENNESE TAPESTRY

If youth knew; if age could.
SIGMUND FREUD

Hertha's Vienna spanned the years between the 1890s through to the end of the 1960s, a most remarkable time in the city's history. The longtime capital of a large multinational empire under the German-speaking Habsburg dynasty for five centuries, Vienna after 1918 became the capital of the small Republic of Austria. With a population of 1.9 million, the city of Vienna housed 28 percent of the country's entire population by 1934. 1900s Vienna was the age of some of the most formidable artists and intellectuals in modern European history, home to a wealth of celebrated writers, artists, musicians and scholars.

Modern Vienna was also a place of unmitigated horrors and tragedy. In 1938, the Jewish population in Vienna was estimated at 170,000 and including those of mixed Jewish-Christian background and converts from Judaism, it may have been as high as 200,000, making up more than 10 percent of the city's inhabitants. Thousands witnessing the looming threat of anti-Semitic sentiment emigrated at this time, including an elderly Dr Sigmund Freud, the inventor of psychoanalytic thought, who in June 1938 left the foreboding doom of his cherished Vienna aboard the Orient Express and moved to Hampstead, London for what was to be the last year of his life.

By the summer of 1939, hundreds of Jewish-owned factories and thousands of businesses had been closed or confiscated by the government who had introduced anti-Jewish legislation to extinguish any cultural or economic growth within the community.

All in all, the SS and police deported some 47,555 Austrian Jews to concentration camps in the east. The vast majority of the deportees, along with approximately 18,000 refugees to Austria, were murdered during the Holocaust. Today the Viennese Jewish population is estimated at around 10,000. No more than 1,000 of them were Holocaust survivors.

From the late-18th through to the mid-19th century, Vienna was the musical capital of Europe. Austrian composers Haydn, Mozart, Schubert, Brahms, Strauss and composer and conductor Gustav Mahler, along with the Vienna Philharmonic and the Vienna Boys Choir, founded in 1498, preceded modern day Vienna. By the arrival of the new century, nothing could eclipse these magnificent forefathers but the new shining stars had become the musicians, conductors, actors and actresses who interpreted their timeless and magical works. Hertha would have surely many times heard Irmgard Seefried, a German soprano of Austrian parentage who in 1943 made her debut at the Vienna State Opera performing as Eva in Wagner's *Die Meistersinger*, and who remained part of its ensemble until her retirement in 1976. With a completely natural delivery, her warm tone and appealing personality made her a much-celebrated star.

Austrian conductors such as Karl Böhm, Herbert von Karajan, Wilhelm Furtwängler and pianists Friedrich Gulda and Alfred Brendel were, by the mid-twentieth century, taking the classical music world by storm and fêted with great reverence in New York, Berlin and London. Von Karajan's obituary in *The New York Times* described him as 'probably the world's best-known conductor and one of the most powerful figures in classical music'.

In art and design, The Vienna Secession, co-founded by Gustav Klimt and Joseph Maria Olbrich, and *Jugendstil* (the German equivalent to *art nouveau*) art movements dominated the age between 1897 and the early 1900s. There were also the city's prominent architectural giants. Otto Wagner designed the Karlsplatz Pavilions, a stylish pair of underground railway exits on the Karlsplatz with sunflower motifs and green copper roofs. His Wagner Pavilions and the Kirche am Steinhof are equally awe-inspiring. Adolf Loos designed in splendid elegance Loos Haus, a fomer tailoring firm and the American Bar in 1908, a tiny space with floors and ceilings feature layers of dark marble and black onyx, making this a dark little gem of a bar quite ahead of its time.

In the early twentieth century, playwright and novelist Arthur Schnitzler shocked audiences when his play *Reigen* was first performed. A series of 10 dialogues, every act focuses on the erotic desires of each of its ten characters. Schnitzler originally only printed 200 copies in 1903 for his fellow writers in the coffeehouses. In 1920 the play was performed for the first time in Hungary as it was banned by the state in Vienna and Leipzig once the nature of the play had been revealed, and therefore could not be

performed at home. It was filmed as *La Ronde* by Max Ophüls in 1950. Stefan Zweig was another highly accomplished writer of the era. Born into the Viennese bourgeoisie in 1881, Zweig won a poetry prize in his ambitious early years and went on to become a prolific and much-translated novelist, essayist, dramatist and librettist, as well as a renowned translator, and the author of a late autobiography, poignantly named *The World of Yesterday*, written while he was in transcontinental flight from the disaster unfolding in central Europe.

Throughout the era, Austria's class system, determined by social status and not necessarily wealth, remained strong among the multi-tiered aristocrats and upper class families within its society. Viennese women of this milieu had an elegant but always understated air with a uniform of conservative grace, impeccably dressed each day in a handmade skirt and blouse (never trousers!), ironed with a gently starched collar and worn with perfectly polished shoes with a moderate heel. For a more formal luncheon, a light woollen suit was often worn, adorned with a tasteful broach. Wearing too much or precious jewellery would be considered vulgar; evening was the time for heirlooms to sparkle. Women in their advanced years would put on their chokers made of small beads woven into a broad band, which would disguise somewhat less youthful necks. Right up to the 1960s, gloves were always worn when stepping out, even during the warm summer months; beautifully handcrafted in ecru or white, crocheted of fine cotton thread, not reaching beyond one's wrist.

My mother recalls a cocktail dress that my grandmother – by nature an excellent seamstress – had made for her in the 1950s, a charming recollection of a strict mother trying to accept her daughter's modern vision:

'Having searched through rolls upon rolls of material in every retail store, I finally discovered the perfect shade and texture of a warm mocha silk duchesse; it took some persuasion for Mami to give her consent. Then, we had to come to the mutual agreement on design: there was not a single pattern suitable for our ideas so Mami would make her own and after many tearful fittings, the outcome of her enduring labour of love was splendid! A simple bodice with a wide decolleté, short sleeves and a skirt, gathered into tiny pleats just below the waistline, reaching mid-calf. Up to this day, I wish that masterpiece was still around; a sweet memory, in the way in which only women can reminisce about certain exquisite pieces from a past wardrobe.'

The little black dress had also made its entry, with the gentle gray flannel dresses being of equal elegance and more often than not worn by the conservative elite. Dressmakers were kept busy either by creating new clothes, or just as frequently making alterations to existing items that would be worn for decades.

The etiquette of a social invitation as seemingly simple as lunch was also steeped in protocol. When invited, most typically for 12.30pm, unwavering punctuality was expected. One would present the hostess with a pretty but, as ever, classic bouquet of flowers or a small bombonière of the finest truffles – as few as two or three was most appropriate as they were sure to be beautifully wrapped from a fine chocolatier. Wine was unheard of as an offering. If flowers were presented, any floral wrapping would be removed before reaching the door. The meal, served on arrival, may have lasted for about an hour, followed by a coffee and small dessert and then leaving your hosts for a *Verdaungschlaf* (digestion nap) shortly after 2pm. Lunches were held during the week as weekends were mostly reserved for family. In the week, offices and shops were closed for business between 12.30pm until 3pm so it was not unusual to see both men and women lunching in this way. With the advent of phones, guests would follow up early the next morning with a gracious call (once phones were commonplace) of appreciation. Phone exchanges remained brief as even local calls were costly. For a larger gathering or special occasion, a handwritten thank you note was posted without delay.

After the Second World War, Vienna was split among the Allies until 1955 when Austria regained its independence. By the end of the 1960s, Vienna had become one of the most sophisticated European old-world cities, drawing thousands to the capital every year. For insiders, no one could specify what had changed, but only that it had.

Vorspeisen

STARTERS

In April 1929, my grandparents were married in the chapel of my grandmother's family home on the outskirts of Ljubljana, Slovenia. The estate, set in a former cloister, was called *Freudenthal*, which loosely translates as 'joyful valley'. It was indeed a very joyous time, as twenty-nine friends and family members, resplendent in their silks, pearls and top hats, were presented with an elegant country menu, prepared by the bustling cooks who ran the large household.

Each guest received a place card. The front of the card features an engagement photo of my grandparents which had been taken in Hertha's atelier in Vienna. The wedding menu is outlined on the inside of the card. The selections are a reflection of food that would have been sophisticated dishes of the era – simple by today's standards but noble in their time. The eight-course menu begins with a soup followed by a fish and mayonnaise entrée before continuing with the meat courses, a salad, ice cream, and finally seasonal fruit, exemplifying the fresh ingredients that were easily available and plentiful.

Starters were traditionally reserved for formal or festive gatherings. In Hertha's recipe collection, she includes egg dishes such as baked béchamel eggs, fish, cold meats and pâtés, and several dishes referred to, even in the German, as *puddings*, a kind of casserole with meat or noodle-based ingredients.

My grandmother kept Hertha's place card, which we found amongst her treasured correspondence after many decades. On the back, the signatures of all the guests remain intact.

Fischröllchen

FISH CROQUETTES

MAKES 24/SERVES 6

FOR THE FISH

1 kg fish of choice, whole or fillets (cod is good)

Sunflower oil, for greasing

Salt and freshly ground pepper

A few sprigs of parsley

1 clove of garlic, peeled

Wedge of fennel (optional)

3 lemon slices

3 sprigs of fresh dill (optional)

1 large egg

2 anchovy fillets, mashed

3 tbsp vegetable oil

½ small onion, peeled and finely chopped

FOR THE BÉCHAMEL SAUCE

170 ml milk

40 g butter

60 g plain flour

Salt

FOR THE COATING

50 g plain flour, seasoned with salt and freshly ground pepper

2 large eggs, lightly beaten

120 g breadcrumbs

300 ml sunflower oil, for frying

Preheat the oven to 180°C/350°F/gas 4.

If using a whole fish, skin and debone it, and cut it into chunks. Place the fish pieces in a shallow, lightly oiled, ovenproof dish. Cover with a sprinkling of salt and pepper, a few sprigs of parsley, the garlic clove and fennel bulb wedge, if using, and the lemon slices. Drizzle with a little more oil. Additional herbs, such as dill, may also be used if desired. Cover with a sheet of aluminium foil and bake for 15–20 minutes.

Remove the fish from the oven and flake it into smallish pieces, using a fork.

To make the béchamel sauce, start by warming the milk in a saucepan. In a separate medium-size saucepan, melt the butter over a medium heat. Stir in the flour which will be quickly absorbed by the butter. Gradually add the warm milk to the flour mixture, stirring vigorously and constantly until all the milk has been used and the mixture comes to a boil – this should take about 5 minutes. When the sauce appears smooth, season with salt and cook for another few minutes, stirring all the time. Remove from heat and set aside to cool. When the sauce has cooled, add the egg and mix in the flaked fish and anchovy fillets.

Heat the vegetable oil in a frying pan and gently fry the onion until golden. Add to the fish mixture and season to taste.

Using your hands, form sausage-shaped croquettes of the fish mixture approximately 7 cm long and 2.5 cm in diameter.

You will need three plates: place the seasoned flour in the first, the lightly beaten eggs in the second and the breadcrumbs in the third. Coat each croquette first in the flour, then in the egg, and lastly in the breadcrumbs.

Preheat the oven to 160°C/325°F/gas 3. Heat the oil in a large frying pan and fry the croquettes in batches until golden brown. Carefully remove them from the pan with kitchen tongs and place on paper towels to drain. Keep the batches warm in the oven, leaving the oven door slightly ajar until all the croquettes have been made.

Gebackene Wurströllchen

DEEP-FRIED SAUSAGE ROLLS

SERVES 4

FOR THE SAUSAGE MEAT

200 g sausages (Polish or any cured sausage of your choice)

2 tsp sunflower oil, for frying

½ small onion, peeled and finely chopped

70 g plain flour

125 ml milk

20 g butter

Pinch of salt

1 large egg yolk, plus ½ a whole egg, if required

1 tsp baking powder

FOR THE COATING

30 g plain flour

1 large egg, lightly beaten

100 g breadcrumbs

170 ml sunflower oil, for frying

Remove the casing from the sausages, and cut them into small pieces. Pulse in a food processor until coarsely chopped.

Heat the oil in a frying pan and gently fry the onion until lightly golden. Set aside.

Sift the flour into a bowl.

Pour the milk into a stainless steel saucepan, add the butter and salt, and slowly bring to the boil, removing from the heat just as it comes to the boil. Immediately beat in the flour, using a wooden spoon. Beat until the mixture is smooth and pulls away from the pan, leaving the pan 'clean'. Return the pan to a very low heat and continue to stir vigorously for another 30 seconds. Remove from the heat and allow to cool slightly.

Add the egg yolk, fried onion, baking powder and ground sausage meat to the pan. If the mixture is too stiff, add half a whole egg, lightly beaten, so that the mixture is still fairly thick and is of the consistency of pliable dough. Shape the dough into sausages 7 cm long and 2.5 cm in diameter.

You will need three plates. Place the flour in the first, the lightly beaten egg in the second and the breadcrumbs in the third. Coat each sausage first in the flour, then in the egg and lastly in the breadcrumbs.

Heat the oil in a heavy-base frying pan and fry the breaded sausages on a medium to high heat until golden on all sides. Carefully remove them from the pan with kitchen tongs and place on paper towels to drain.

Gefüllte Eier à la Christoph

STUFFED EGGS À LA CHRISTOPH

SERVES 6

6 large eggs

2 tsp salt

2–3 tbsp mayonnaise,
to taste

2–3 tsp Dijon mustard,
to taste

6–12 drops Tabasco sauce

Paprika, for dusting

Make sure the eggs are at room temperature. Fill a pan large enough to comfortably hold the eggs with cold water, and carefully place the eggs in the pan. Add the salt to the water (this will help with peeling them later) and bring the water to a rapid boil. At that point, remove the pan from the heat and let the eggs sit in the pan, covered, for 30 minutes exactly. This will hard-boil the eggs without overcooking them and leaving an unattractive grey edge around the yolk.

Rinse the eggs in ice cold water. Once the eggs have cooled to room temperature, peel them.

Slice the eggs in half lengthways and carefully transfer the yolks into a mixing bowl (try very gently pinching the base of the egg and the yolk will come out quite easily). Mash the yolks with a fork and mix in the mayonnaise, mustard and Tabasco sauce.

Fill the halved egg whites with the yolk mixture using either a teaspoon or a piping bag fitted with a large nozzle. Sprinkle with paprika. The eggs can be made in advance and refrigerated. Remove from the fridge 30 minutes before serving. Keeps for up to two days.

NOTE
The quantities for the mayonnaise, mustard and Tabasco sauce depend on taste and your own preference for the consistency of the filling. We don't like it too runny, so we use the lower quantity of mayonnaise. For a bit of extra bite, use the higher quantities of mustard and Tabasco sauce.

Käseauflauf

CHEESE SOUFFLÉ

SERVES 4

20 g unsalted butter

60 g plain flour

500 ml full-fat milk

200 g Emmental cheese, grated

½ tsp salt

3 large egg yolks

4 large egg whites

½ tsp paprika

Butter for greasing soufflé dish

Preheat the oven to 200°C/400°F/gas 6.

Heat the butter in a saucepan on a medium heat and stir in the flour using a wooden spoon. Gradually add the milk while stirring steadily. The mixture will at first appear a little lumpy, and at this stage you may wish swap your wooden spoon for a whisk. Whisk constantly until the milk comes to a boil. Boil for a few minutes, stirring all the while, until you get a smooth sauce.

Remove the pan from heat and stir in the grated cheese. Return the pan to a medium heat and bring the mixture back to the boil, then remove from the heat. Season with salt and set aside to cool. Once cooled, beat in the egg yolks, one at a time, and add a dash of paprika.

In a bowl, whisk the egg whites until stiff and fold them into the mixture. Grease a 22-cm round ovenproof dish, pour in the mixture, and bake for 15 minutes (check the soufflé without opening the oven door at this point and if it has not risen, leave for another few minutes), then lower the oven temperature to 180°C/350°F/gas 4, and bake for another 5 minutes. Don't expect the dish to rise as high as a standard French-style soufflé – it is a less elevated but equally tasty affair. Serve immediately.

Schinkenkipferln

CRESCENTS WITH HAM FILLING

MAKES 12/SERVES 4

FOR THE DOUGH

100 g medium-size floury potatoes

100 g plain flour, plus extra for dusting

100 g butter, chilled and cut into chunks

1 tsp salt, or less if the ham is very salty

FOR THE FILLING

150 g smoked ham

50 g bacon

1 large egg white

Wash and steam the potatoes in a steamer rather than in water; this will prevent the potatoes from absorbing too much water and becoming mushy. Drain and cool.

Once cooled, peel the potatoes and press them through a potato ricer. Flour your work surface, keeping a liberal amount of extra flour to hand.

Pour the flour onto the work surface and add the chunks of butter to it. Add the cold pressed potatoes and the salt and work everything together as quickly as possible to form a smooth dough. Shape the dough into a ball and refrigerate for 30 minutes.

Meanwhile, line a baking tray with baking parchment and preheat the oven to 230°C/450°F/gas 8. While the oven is heating up, make the filling. Chop the ham and bacon into cubes, place in a food processor and pulse until fairly fine. Set aside.

Take half of the dough (keeping the other half in the fridge) and roll it out onto a well-floured surface to 1 cm thick. This will require frequent turning and dusting with a liberal amount of flour, so that it does not stick to the surface.

Cut into 12-cm squares, place a heaped tablespoon of the ham/bacon mixture into the centre of each square. Fold one corner diagonally over the mixture to the other corner and press down to seal. Pinch the remaining two corners together and along the seams and fold them towards each other, to form a crescent shape. Lift each crescent onto the baking sheet. Brush egg white evenly over the crescents and bake for 25–30 minutes, until golden brown. Repeat with remaining dough and proceed as above. These crescents taste best eaten immediately, while still warm.

Suppen und Einlagen

SOUPS AND ACCOMPANIMENTS

The presence of a freshly made soup at a Viennese table cannot be underestimated. Many years ago, my great-uncle Bruno had been invited to a formal gathering where an elaborate meal was served. When he returned home, his wife asked about the meeting, eager to hear who had attended and what had been served. 'Everything was very good, but the most important thing was missing.' 'Oh, and what was this?' enquired my aunt with great curiosity. 'The soup,' declared Uncle Bruno with even greater conviction.

A soup is just as important a course as the main dish; it needs to be just right. A more formal meal always begins with soup. It is presented at the table in an elegant soup terrine. A matching *service* (dinner set) of fine porcelain soup plates — much shallower than ordinary soup bowls — allow just the right amount to be served. Second helpings are never offered (and certainly never requested!) and despite the presence of beautiful salt and pepper servers, it would be considered disrespectful to your hostess to add another pinch or two.

Dunkle Rindsuppe

BEEF CONSOMMÉ

MAKES 2 LITRES

2 kg beef bones

1 large onion, peeled and quartered

2 large carrots, peeled and cut into 2.5-cm chunks

40 g parsley root, sliced

40 g celeriac, coarsely chopped

½ parsnip, roughly chopped (optional)

2 celery stalks, including the leaves, cut into 5-cm pieces

Green tops of 2 leeks, sliced into 5-cm lengths

3 sprigs parsley

1 large tomato, coarsely chopped

3 bay leaves

1 tbsp salt

½ tsp dried thyme or 1 sprig of fresh thyme

10 peppercorns

1 clove of garlic, peeled

Preheat the oven to 200°C/400°F/gas 6.

Wipe the bones with a moist paper towel and place them in a roasting pan. Roast for 50–60 minutes, turning regularly, until they begin to brown and start rendering fat.

Add the onion, carrots, parsley root, celeriac and parsnip to the pan, and brown for about 15 minutes. Watch that they do not become too dark!

Transfer the contents of the roasting pan into a large pot, discarding the fat from the pan, and set aside.

Place the roasting pan on the hob over a medium heat. Pour in 115 ml cold water, scraping and stirring vigorously, and bring the liquid to a boil. Remove from the heat and add this liquid to the large pot with the remaining ingredients. Add just over 3 litres of water and bring to the boil, uncovered. Immediately reduce the heat and simmer gently, covered, for 3–4 hours.

Strain and taste the stock. If the flavour is not strong enough, boil for a little longer, uncovered, until the juice becomes more concentrated.

Grießnockerln

SEMOLINA DUMPLINGS

SERVES 4

50 g butter, at room temperature

2 large eggs

150 g coarse semolina

½ tsp salt

Put the butter in a bowl and whisk until creamed, using an electric mixer. Adding one egg at a time, continue whisking so that the mixture becomes light and fluffy. Add the semolina, salt and 2 tablespoons of water, and mix by hand until the batter is well blended. Set aside for 1 hour.

In a large pan, bring a generous amount of salted water to the boil. Take a teaspoon of the batter and use a second teaspoon to cup the batter and round out the dumpling, to create an even oval shape. Work quickly and drop the dumplings into the boiling water until all the batter has been used up. Reduce the temperature to a simmer and cook for 8–10 minutes, then remove the pan from heat and let the dumplings stand in the water for another 5 minutes.

These dumplings are traditionally added to a good beef stock, such as the Beef consommé on page 42 just before serving.

Lebernockerln

LIVER DUMPLINGS IN BEEF CONSOMMÉ

SERVES 4

2 stale bread rolls

150 g calves liver

2 tbsp butter or lard

1 small onion, peeled and finely chopped

1 clove of garlic, peeled and minced

3 tbsp finely chopped flat-leaf parsley

Pinch of dried marjoram

Pinch of freshly ground pepper

½ tsp salt

1 large egg

50 g fine fresh breadcrumbs

1 litre beef stock

Chopped chives, to garnish

Cut the bread rolls into thin slices and pour over approximately 115 ml cold water to soften them. Mince the liver: a food processor with a blade attachment works well; pulse, rather than blend on a constant speed.

Melt the butter (or other fat) and fry the onion with the garlic until transparent. Add the parsley and remove the pan from the heat.

Squeeze the excess water from the rolls. Crumble the softened rolls into the onion mixture and add all remaining ingredients (minus the beef stock and chopped chives), mixing well. If the mixture appears too soft, add a few more breadcrumbs. Set aside for 20 minutes, then form the mixture into 3–4 cm balls (make sure your hands are wet to avoid the mixture sticking to them).

Bring the beef stock to the boil and gently ease the dumplings into the boiling stock. Reduce the heat to a simmer and cover as soon as the liquid begins to come to another boil. Barely simmer for about 15 minutes.

Spoon the dumplings into soup plates and then pour the beef stock over them. Garnish with chopped chives.

Krensuppe

CREAM OF HORSERADISH SOUP

SERVES 4

400 g floury potatoes

2 medium onions

40 g butter

450 ml clear vegetable stock, made from a vegetable cube

225 ml low-sodium chicken stock, homemade or canned

250 ml whipping cream

1 large egg yolk

2 tbsp white wine

40 g fresh horseradish, very finely grated (use a zester)

Salt and freshly ground pepper

Freshly chopped dill, to garnish

Wash, peel and cut the potatoes into 1 cm cubes and coarsely chop the onions. Heat the butter in a large stockpot over a low to medium heat until bubbling. Add the potatoes and the onions, and increase the heat to medium, stirring occasionally until the onions turn just translucent, but not mushy and certainly not browned.

Add the vegetable and chicken stocks to the pot, cover and bring to a boil. Reduce the heat to low-medium and simmer until the potatoes are tender, which should take about 20 minutes.

Remove the pot from the heat and purée the contents directly in the pot using a hand-held blender. Return the pot to a medium heat and stir in the whipping cream, increasing the heat a little to bring to a gentle but not rolling boil. Now remove from the heat. In a bowl, whisk the egg yolk with the wine and stir into the hot soup.

Finally, stir in the horseradish and season to taste, but do test the soup first, since the stock may already contain enough salt. Serve hot and sprinkle the chopped dill over each soup plate.

NOTE

For a decadent and stylish touch, pour whipped cream into ice cube trays and freeze. Remove when the soup is being served, adding one iced 'dollop' per serving.

Linsensuppe

LENTIL SOUP

SERVES 6

2 tbsp vegetable oil

40 g smoked bacon, diced

2 medium carrots, cut into
1 cm cubes

1 leek, white part only,
rinsed and sliced

20 g celeriac, cut into 1 cm
cubes

20 g parsley root, cubed

¼ parsnip, peeled and cubed

100 g Puy lentils, rinsed

½ tsp salt

1 tbsp fresh flat-leaf parsley,
finely chopped

Freshly ground pepper

680 ml chicken stock,
preferably homemade

1 tsp (or more, to taste)
freshly squeezed lemon juice

OPTIONAL

100 g Frankfurter sausages,
cooked gently (do not boil or
they will burst), skinned and
cut into 2.5 cm slices

Pour the oil into a large stockpot and heat over a medium to
high heat. Add the bacon and cook for about 2 minutes, stirring
regularly, until the bacon becomes crisp, but not brown.

Stir in the cubed/sliced root vegetables. Sauté for 2 minutes,
until the vegetables begin to soften. Add the lentils, salt, flat-leaf
parsley and a few grindings of pepper. Cover and reduce the heat to
low to medium. Sauté for another 5 to 8 minutes, checking to make
sure that the mixture isn't sticking to the bottom of the pot.

Uncover, pour in the chicken stock along with 450 ml water,
and bring to the boil. Cover again and allow the soup to simmer for
about 1¼ hours, until the lentils are cooked.

Remove the pot from the heat and allow to cool slightly before
puréeing two-thirds of the soup in a blender for a smoother
consistency. Return the puréed soup to the stockpot with the
remaining unblended soup. Add lemon juice to taste and if desired,
the Frankfurters. At this point, the consistency of the soup may need
adjusting and a little more water added for a thinner soup. The soup
will keep refrigerated in an airtight container for several days.
When reheating, do so over a medium rather than high heat.

Schwammerlsuppe

CREAM OF MUSHROOM SOUP

SERVES 4

FOR THE MUSHROOMS

20 g butter

½ medium onion, peeled and very finely chopped

1 clove of garlic, peeled and minced

2 heaped tbsp finely chopped parsley

150 g fresh mushrooms, very thinly sliced (white button mushrooms are standard but a mix of chanterelles and porcini is best)

FOR THE ROUX

2 tbsp dried wild mushrooms (a combination of chanterelles and porcini is ideal)

4 tbsp butter

4 tbsp plain flour

Salt and freshly ground pepper

4 tbsp soured cream

To prepare the mushrooms, melt the butter over a medium heat in a large, heavy-base frying pan until bubbling. Add the onion and garlic, and stir gently until the onion is translucent but not yet beginning to colour. Add the parsley and the mushrooms, stirring to coat evenly. Fry over a low to medium heat until all the moisture has evaporated. Set aside but do not cover with a lid.

To make the roux, pulse the dried wild mushrooms in a clean coffee grinder. Transfer to a heatproof bowl and pour over 225 ml of boiling water and soak for 30 minutes.

Melt the butter in a large stockpot over a medium to high heat until it begins to bubble. Add the flour all in one go and stir until it begins to foam. Now add just under 1 litre of boiling water, one cup at a time, while stirring vigorously to avoid any lumps from forming. Continue in this manner until all the water has been used. Add the dried mushrooms and the juice they have been soaking in. Increase the heat to bring the soup to a rolling boil, then reduce to a simmer, cover the pot with a well-fitting lid, and cook for 30 minutes.

Now add the fried mushrooms to the stockpot and cook on a low simmer for another 15 minutes. If the soup is too thin, remove the lid and simmer for a little longer. Season to taste with salt and pepper (if the salt is added too soon, the mushrooms can become rubbery).

In a small bowl, take 3 tablespoons of the soup and mix it with the soured cream to create a smooth paste. Stir it into the pot with a whisk, without bringing the soup back to the boil. Serve hot. This soup will keep for two days in the fridge.

NOTE
Never wash mushrooms under running water – always wipe them with damp kitchen paper. If using button mushrooms, trim the stems to about 1 cm below the cap.

Fleisch und Fische

MEAT AND FISH

Meat has always played a significant role in Viennese cuisine. The Austro-Hungarian Monarchy or Empire, which formed in 1867 and lasted until 1918, spanned modern-day Austria, Hungary, Bohemia, Moravia, Slovakia, and parts of Poland, Romania, Slovenia, Croatia and Italy. Vienna was one of the two capital cities of the Monarchy and the dishes influenced by these many cultures made their way to Hertha's cookbook and continue to remain at the heart of Viennese cooking today. *Szegediner Goulash* (see page 58), originating from Hungary; the famed *Wiener Schnitzel* (see page 61), widely believed to have stemmed from Italy in the 15th or 16th century; and fish dishes named Yugoslavian Fish and Tuna Fish *Brodetto* (meaning 'little broth' in Italian), taste divine and are reminders of a flavourful, culturally-rich past.

Founded in 1848, the St Marx slaughterhouse in the centre of Vienna received live cattle of primarily pork and beef from Hungary and Serbia. By the time it reached the butcher, standing orders from upper-class households were in place, with servants regularly fetching the orders for the next few days. A beef bouillon would be prepared almost daily, simmering on the stove from early morning.

Arabisches Reiterfleisch

ARABIAN MEATLOAF

SERVES 4

150 g minced beef

1 small onion, peeled and very finely chopped

1 small gherkin, finely chopped

2 apples, peeled and cut into small cubes

2 tsp grated fresh horseradish

3 tsp tomato purée

Salt and freshly ground pepper

Paprika

1 tsp sugar

1 large egg

30 g butter

225 ml soured cream

Preheat to the oven to 190°C/375°F/gas 5.

Mix all the ingredients together in a bowl, except for the butter and the soured cream.

Melt the butter on a medium to high heat in a 25-cm cast-iron ovenproof frying pan until it begins to bubble (but not brown), then remove from heat. A frying pan gives a better result as the edges of the meatloaf become crusty and more flavourful.

Place the mixture into the hot butter and pat it down so that it is evenly distributed in the pan. Transfer the pan to the preheated oven and bake for 40 to 45 minutes, until it is nicely browned. Remove from the oven and pour the soured cream over the top and cook for another 10 minutes. Despite its exotic name, this is a simple, almost rustic dish, nicely complemented with rice and a green salad.

Literally translated, *Arabisches Reiterfleisch* means 'Arabian horseman's meat'. It was a dish invented and popularised in the 1950s by Germany's first TV chef, Clemens Wilmenrod. Tante Hertha was likely not a regular TV watcher in 1953 when the programme first aired, but nevertheless, the recipe charmingly found its way into her cookbook.

Gerollte Rindschnitzel

ROLLED BEEFSTEAK

**SERVES 6
(MAKES 8 ROLLS)**

1 kg boneless sirloin or
rib-eye steak, cut into 1-cm
slices at the butcher

Salt and freshly ground
pepper

50 g spicy pork sausage meat

50 g 'lardo di colonnata'
(streaky bacon will do)

50 g gherkins

60 g butter

100 ml light corn oil

1 medium onion, peeled
and finely chopped

2 tbsp flour

250 ml soured cream

Pound the meat with a tenderiser until very thin. Score each slice at the edges. Season each side liberally with salt and pepper. Now spread a thin layer of sausage meat (squeezing it out of the casing) on top of each piece, as if you were buttering bread.

Cut the bacon and pickles into thin strips. Place a few strips of bacon and pickles lengthways at the base of each slice of meat and roll up tightly, securing both ends with string so that the rolls hold their shape.

Heat the butter and oil together in a frying pan over a medium to high heat, making sure the fat does not start to smoke. Add as many rolls as will fit the pan and brown evenly on all sides. When all the pieces have been browned, transfer them to a large saucepan and set aside.

Turn the heat down a little and add the onion to the frying pan (you may need to add a little more fat) and fry to a rich golden colour. Now add enough cold water to just barely cover the onions. As soon as they are brought to a boil, pour the onions and water over the meat rolls in the saucepan. Cover with a lid and simmer on a low heat for 45 minutes—1 hour, until the meat is tender. Check periodically, and if necessary, add small quantities of water. The meat should be braising in its own juice so be sure to add water very sparingly. When cooked, remove the rolls from the pan (but reserve the juice) and arrange them on a serving platter. Keep warm in a low oven while preparing the gravy.

To make the gravy, mix the flour with the soured cream and add it to the reserved pan juices and bring to a gentle boil, stirring all the time. Reduce the heat and continue stirring regularly for another 10—15 minutes. If the sauce becomes too thick, add a little more water so that the consistency is more like a gravy rather than a thick béchamel-style sauce. Remove from the heat. Strain the sauce through a sieve into a bowl, pressing the sauce through the strainer with the back of a metal spoon. Season to taste.

Remove the meat rolls from the oven and pour some of the sauce over them and the rest into a saucière for the dinner table. Serve with boiled new potatoes or *Semmelknödeln* (see page 94), a typical Austrian dumpling.

Szegediner Gulyás

SZEGEDINER GOULASH

SERVES 6

1 kg sauerkraut

110 g smoked speck (cured fatty bacon)

1 tsp sunflower oil

4 medium onions, peeled and finely chopped

1 tbsp paprika

1 heaped tsp caraway seeds

Salt

A little chicken stock

½ green pepper, cut into thin strips

1 kg shoulder or belly pork

2 tbsp lard or butter

1 clove of garlic, peeled and crushed

1 tbsp paprika

½ tomato, chopped

½ tsp black peppercorns

2 tsp plain flour

125 ml soured cream

Drain the liquid from the sauerkraut and reserve the juice.

Cut the smoked speck into 1-cm cubes. Heat the oil in a heavy-base casserole and gently fry the pancetta on a medium heat. Add two of the onions and fry until golden. Remove from heat, add the paprika and caraway seeds, stir and return to the heat, adding the drained sauerkraut with a pinch of salt. Add a little chicken stock so that it just covers the bottom of the casserole dish. Cover and simmer over a low heat for approximately 50 minutes. During this time, check that the dish hasn't dried out (if it's looking a little dry, add a little more chicken stock but make sure there isn't too much liquid), then add the green pepper strips and cook for another 10 minutes.

Meanwhile, cut the pork into 2.5-cm cubes and season with salt. In a separate heavy-base casserole, melt the lard or butter and gently fry the remaining two onions until softened and then add the garlic. Reduce the heat, add the paprika, then add the pork and season with salt. Brown in batches rather than all at once. Return all the meat to the casserole and add the tomato, peppercorns and just enough water or chicken stock to prevent burning. Reduce the heat to very low, stir in the flour to coat the meat, and simmer for about 1 hour, until the meat is tender. Add a little more water or chicken stock only if absolutely necessary: the less additional liquid added the better, so that the meat is essentially swimming in its own juices.

Now combine the sauerkraut with the meat and stir lightly. Add the soured cream before serving, making sure not to mix it in completely: a few streaks of soured cream should remain.

NOTE

If pressed for time, you can prepare the first step of the recipe a day in advance. The flavours improve over time with this dish, making any leftovers even more tasty. If reheating, warm on a gentle heat without letting it come to a boil.

Wiener Schnitzel

WIENER SCHNITZEL

SERVES 4

50 g plain flour

2 large eggs, lightly beaten

100 g breadcrumbs

4 × 150 g veal cutlets (you
could also use pork or
chicken fillets)

1 tsp salt

Lard or oil, for frying

Lemon wedges, to serve

You will need three plates: place the flour in the first, the lightly
beaten eggs in the second and the breadcrumbs in the third.

Pound each cutlet with a meat tenderizer to a thickness of 5 mm.
With a sharp knife, make small cuts every 2.5 cm around the edges
of the meat: this ensures that the meat will stay flat and not curl up
when frying. Season both sides with salt and set aside.

Coat both sides of each cutlet first in the flour, then in the egg,
and lastly in the breadcrumbs. When turning the cutlets over in the
breadcrumbs, do not pat down the crumbs or the crispiness of the
coating will be lost in the frying process.

The best and most authentic taste for frying is lard, but any oil
(except olive oil) can be used instead. Heat the lard or oil in a frying
pan on medium-high heat and fry the cutlets for 2–3 minutes on
each side until golden, gently shaking the pan. Make sure there is
always enough fat in the pan so that the cutlets do not stick to the
surface. Remove and drain on paper towels.

This dish is always served with a wedge of lemon alongside.
A cucumber salad and/or potato salad are traditional and delicious
accompaniments.

Though synonymous with the idea of Viennese cuisine, Tante
Hertha did not have this dish in her cookbook. For *Wiener Schnitzel*,
one would go to the local *Wirtshaus*, a kind of countrified pub where
simple but delicious fresh dishes are served. Every Austrian knows
how to prepare this specialty by heart, which likely explains the
absence of a documented recipe. Nonetheless, it remains a must-have
in the Viennese repertoire so we are including it, by heart, here.

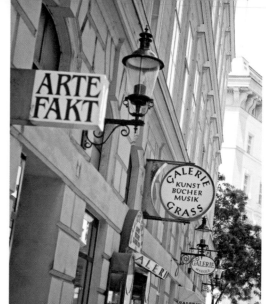

Wurzelfleisch
Sharon Schauenstein

PORK ROAST WITH ROOT VEGETABLES

SERVES 4

1 kg shoulder of pork

1 tsp salt

1 tsp caraway seeds

1 glove of garlic, peeled and chopped

2 tbsp corn oil

100 g carrots, peeled and finely sliced

100 g celeriac, peeled and cut into ½-cm slices

100 g parsley root, peeled and cut into ½-cm slices

100 g parsnips, peeled and finely sliced

Onion, peeled and cut into ½-cm slices

Preheat to the oven to 160°C/325°F/gas 3.

In a small bowl, mix the salt with the caraway seeds and garlic into a paste and rub into the surface of the meat.

In a frying pan, heat the oil and sear the meat on all sides for 2–3 minutes until lightly browned. Now transfer the meat to a roasting pan. Cook for 1 hour, basting the meat with its own juices from time to time.

After 1 hour, turn the meat and arrange the prepared vegetables around the roast. Cook for another 1–1½ hours. During this time, check that the meat isn't drying out by adding small amounts of water if necessary (it should not be swimming in liquid though). You will end up with colourfully glazed vegetables and a tender, tasty meat dish.

To serve, transfer the meat and vegetables to a warmed serving dish and cut into thin slices. For a hearty meal, *Semmelknödeln* (see page 94) can also be served as a side dish.

Fisch im Bierteig

BEER-BATTERED FISH

SERVES 6

FOR THE FISH

6 x 150-g white fish fillets of your choice (such as cod or haddock)

Salt

Juice of 1 lemon

FOR THE BATTER

180 g plain flour

1 tsp salt

180 ml beer

1 tbsp oil

2 large egg yolks

2–3 large egg whites

Light vegetable oil, for frying

Lemon wedges, to garnish

Season the fish pieces on both sides with salt and sprinkle sparingly with the lemon juice.

To make the batter, beat the flour, salt, beer, oil and egg yolks together in a bowl to a smooth batter using an electric mixer. Set the batter aside to rest for 30 minutes.

Just before the 30 minutes are up, whisk the egg whites until stiff. Fold them swiftly and gently into the beer batter.

Heat the oil in a large heavy-based pan or deep-fat fryer until a cube of stale bread turns golden in 30 seconds. Reduce the heat a little, then dip the fish into the batter and fry in the hot oil on both sides until golden brown. Drain on paper towels. Serve with new potatoes in butter and freshly chopped flat-leaf parsley.

Jugoslawischer Fisch
YUGOSLAVIAN FISH

SERVES 2–3

500 g filleted white fish of your choice (such as cod, haddock or trout), cut into large chunks

1 large onion, peeled and very finely chopped

1 clove of garlic, peeled and crushed

100 g tomato purée

200 ml whipping cream

Salt

½ tsp peppercorns

1 tsp paprika

1 large egg yolk

Gewürze nach Geschmack (this translates as 'seasoning of your choice'. Tante Hertha wasn't specific, so use your favourite spices to complement the fish, such as light paprika, tarragon, thyme or freshly chopped flat leaf parsley)

40 g cold butter, plus extra for greasing

30 g freshly grated Parmesan cheese

Preheat to the oven to 190°C/375°F/gas 5.

In a bowl, mix the fish and all the other ingredients together, (minus the cold butter and cheese).

Generously butter an ovenproof baking dish and pour in the fish mixture. Sprinkle a liberal amount of grated Parmesan cheese over the top. Top off with shavings of butter (make sure the butter is really cold). Bake for 20–25 minutes until golden. Serve with boiled rice.

Hausgemachte Mayonnaise

HOMEMADE MAYONNAISE

MAKES 150 ML

2 large egg yolks

½ tsp salt

125 ml sunflower oil

2 tsp fresh lemon juice,
to taste

½ tsp Worcestershire sauce

½–1 tsp Dijon mustard, or
to taste

Few drops of Tabasco sauce

Pinch of sugar

Pinch of cayenne pepper

Freshly ground white pepper

Put the egg yolks in a mixing bowl with the salt. Place a folded damp kitchen cloth underneath the bowl to prevent it from sliding.

Using a medium-size balloon whisk, whisk the egg yolks. To begin with, add the oil drop by drop, whisking all the time (you can use a turkey baster to ensure the oil is added slowly). The drop-by-drop approach will provide the right texture so that the mayonnaise is firm and not too runny.

As the consistency begins to thicken, you can add the oil in a thin trickle, whisking all the time. Stop every now and then in between each trickle to make sure the oil is properly incorporated. Once the texture becomes quite thick and you have used half the oil, whisk in the lemon juice. Trickle in the remaining oil until it is all incorporated. Using a spoon, mix in the Worcestershire sauce, mustard, Tabasco sauce, sugar, cayenne pepper and pepper, to taste. Transfer to a clean airtight glass jar. Keep refrigerated for up to one week.

NOTE
Keep all ingredients and utensils at room temperature. A cold bowl will prevent the mayonnaise from thickening.

Kräutersauce

HERB SAUCE

MAKES 100 ML

FOR THE MAYONNAISE

1 large egg yolk

90 ml sunflower oil

2–3 tsp lemon juice

Freshly ground pepper

Pinch of mild curry powder

½ tsp caster sugar

Dash of Worcestershire sauce

FOR THE ANCHOVY PASTE

2 anchovy fillets, finely chopped

1 tsp Dijon mustard

1 liberal handful of baby spinach

Half a handful of flat-leaf parsley

Half a handful of dill

Half a handful of chives

Half a handful of lemon thyme

2–3 leaves of mint

1 tsp coarsely chopped capers

2–3 tsp soured cream

Start by making the mayonnaise. Using a medium-size balloon whisk, whisk the egg yolk. To begin with, add the oil drop by drop, whisking all the time (you can use a turkey baster to ensure the oil is added slowly). The drop-by-drop approach will provide the right texture so that the mayonnaise is firm and not too runny.

As the consistency begins to thicken, you can add the oil in a thin trickle, whisking all the time. Stop every now and then in between each trickle to make sure the oil is properly incorporated. Once the texture becomes quite thick and you have used half the oil, whisk in the lemon juice. Trickle in the remaining oil until it is all incorporated. Using a spoon, mix in a grinding of pepper, the curry powder, sugar and Worcestershire sauce. Set aside.

Now make the anchovy paste. In a separate small bowl, mash the anchovies into a smooth paste with the back of a spoon and then stir into the mayonnaise (tinned anchovies taste much better than ready-made anchovy paste, so avoid this shortcut). Mix in the mustard.

Pulse the spinach and all the herbs in a food processor until smooth but not quite a paste. Add the capers and pulse to a paste.

Place a sieve over the bowl of mayonnaise and transfer the herb paste to the sieve. Press the paste through the sieve with the back of a metal spoon, turning it a lovely pale green colour. Stop half-way through to stir in the herb juices into the mayonnaise to make sure that the mayonnaise is not becoming too runny. The end result should be a fairly thick sauce, just like mayonnaise. Adjust the seasoning, if necessary, and finally mix in the soured cream. Transfer to a clean airtight glass jar. Keep refrigerated for up to five days.

This sauce is delicious served with fish and fried meats and is particularly good with pan-fried wild trout.

Sardellensauce

ANCHOVY SAUCE

MAKES 150 ML

125 ml oil (use the oil from
the anchovies and top up with
sunflower oil)

6 tinned anchovies in oil,
finely chopped

1 tbsp capers, finely chopped

2 heaped tbsp very finely
chopped flat-leaf parsley

1–2 tsp lemon juice

Heat 3 tablespoons of the oil in a saucepan over a medium heat.
Add the chopped anchovies and stir until the anchovies form a
smooth paste. Add the remaining oil and heat until it bubbles.
Mix in the capers and parsley, and 1 teaspoon of the lemon juice.
Add the second teaspoon cautiously, according to taste. Remove from
the heat. This sauce makes a perfect accompaniment to roast meat.

Schnittlauchsauce

CHIVE SAUCE

MAKES 300 ML

2 stale white bread rolls

Vinegar water (6 tbsp water
to 3 tbsp mild white wine
vinegar)

2 large egg yolks

½ tsp salt

125 ml oil (half sunflower oil
and half light olive oil)

1–2 tsp lemon juice, to taste
(use more than 1 tsp if
necessary)

6 tbsp finely chopped chives

Dash or two of
Worcestershire sauce

1 tsp or more Dijon mustard,
to taste

Few drops of Tabasco sauce

½ tsp sugar

Freshly ground pepper

3 medium hard-boiled eggs,
roughly chopped

4 tbsp soured cream

Use a grater to remove the crusts from the rolls. Cut the dough into 1 cm cubes. Pour the vinegar water over the bread, cover, and marinate for about 15 minutes.

Put the egg yolks in a mixing bowl with the salt. Place a folded damp kitchen cloth underneath the bowl to prevent it from sliding.

Using a medium-size balloon whisk, whisk the egg yolks. To begin with, add the oil drop by drop, whisking all the time (you can use a turkey baster to ensure the oil is added slowly). The drop-by-drop approach will provide the right texture so that the mayonnaise is firm and not too runny.

As the consistency begins to thicken, you can add the oil in a thin trickle, whisking all the time. Stop every now and then in between each trickle to make sure the oil is properly incorporated. Once the texture becomes quite thick (and you have used half the oil, whisk in the lemon juice. You can then trickle in the remaining oil until it is all incorporated. Using a spoon, mix in the chives, along with Worcestershire sauce, mustard, Tabasco sauce, sugar and pepper, to taste. Set aside.

Squeeze any excess liquid out of the bread. In a food processor, add the bread along with the chopped hard-boiled eggs and pulse until puréed. Mix the puréed bread mixture into the mayonnaise with the soured cream. Transfer to a clean airtight glass jar. Keep refrigerated for up to one week.

Classically served with *Rindfleisch* (boiled beef), it also serves as a wonderful complement to any white fish.

Gesalzene Mehlspeisen

MAINS

Gesalzene Mehlspeisen have a place all of their own in any Austrian cookbook or menu. These savoury, primarily meat-free dishes, are not prepared for formal occasions but rather as a light lunch or dinner, or on a given Friday when meat was traditionally not eaten. Because of their less formal nature, these all-in-one dishes are served among family or close friends only. Some favourite recipes however, such as *Heidensterz* (see page 75), take a certain amount of skill to prepare to perfection and because of this, rise to an elevated status as dishes requested for special occasions, perhaps during a family ski holiday or by a young student returning home for half term.

In grander times, landowners' daughters would have been sent to finishing school so they could teach the cooks — often girls from small villages — how to make these beloved dishes. The regional dishes were ones the girls would have likely already known, having inherited the recipes from their own mothers on the farms. Now as then, a local *Gasthaus* (tavern) offers such specialities, with regional favourites varying across the nine provinces of Austria.

Gemüseauflauf

MIXED VEGETABLE SOUFFLÉ

SERVES 4

FOR THE VEGETABLES

125 g fresh green peas

250 g Brussels sprouts, halved

½ head cauliflower, cut into small rosettes

100 g carrots, peeled and cubed

50 g mushrooms of your choice (chanterelles are best), sliced

20 g butter

FOR THE BÉCHAMEL

60 g butter

60 g plain flour

375 ml full-fat milk, warmed

Salt

4 large eggs, separated

Butter, for greasing

Preheat the oven to 180°C/350°F/gas 4.

Start by preparing the vegetables. Boil all the vegetables (except the mushrooms) in salted water until tender, then drain. Heat the butter in a saucepan and fry the mushrooms, uncovered, stirring regularly until all the liquid has evaporated, then remove from the heat. Set aside the vegetables and prepare the béchamel.

To make the béchamel, melt the butter in a saucepan over a medium heat. Stir in the flour which will be quickly absorbed by the butter. Pour in the warmed milk gradually, stirring all the time, until all the milk has been used and the mixture comes to a light boil: this should take about 5 minutes. When the sauce appears smooth, lower the heat and season with salt. Cook for another 2 minutes, stirring continuously but with less vigour. This should result in a fairly thick, smooth sauce. Remove from heat and set aside to cool.

Once cooled, stir the egg yolks and the prepared vegetables into the béchamel. In a separate clean bowl, whisk the egg whites until they form stiff peaks, then gently fold them into the vegetable and sauce mixture. Transfer into a greased ovenproof casserole and bake, uncovered, for 45 minutes. Serve with a tomato salad.

Heidensterz

BUCKWHEAT CRUMBLE

SERVES 4

250 g organic buckwheat flour

½ tsp salt

80 g lard or butter (the authentic recipes use lard)

In a large frying pan on low heat, dry-roast the buckwheat flour for about 10 minutes, stirring gently, until all the moisture has evaporated.

In a saucepan, bring 285 ml water to the boil with the salt. Add the roasted buckwheat flour to the pan all at once. Cover and reduce the heat to low, and steep for about 10 minutes.

In the meantime, heat the lard or butter in a large, deep saucepan until it begins to bubble. Remove from the heat, then stir it into the buckwheat using a wooden spoon. Cover and allow to set in the pan, until ready to serve. Though known throughout Austria, this dish is traditionally served in the provinces of Styria and Carinthia, with a sauce of freshly picked wild mushrooms.

Herrentorte

GENTLEMAN'S TORTE

SERVES 6

FOR THE BASE

200 g butter, plus extra for greasing

1 large egg

250 g curd cheese (or Austrian *Topfen* if available), sieved

300 g plain flour, sifted, plus extra for flouring

1 tsp baking powder, sifted

1 tsp salt

FOR THE FILLING

100 g butter

110 g Camembert cheese, cut into small chunks

500 g curd cheese, sieved

1 tsp fresh horseradish, grated

1 tsp sugar

2 tbsp finely chopped chives

Salt and freshly ground pepper

2 tbsp finely chopped flat-leaf parsley

150 g black forest ham, chopped

FOR THE TOPPING AND DECORATION

1 slice of pumpernickel bread (optional)

A few slices of salami

3 medium hard-boiled eggs, sliced

A few green olives

A few radishes

Curly parsley, to garnish

Preheat to the oven to 190°C/375°F/gas 5.

Start by making the base. In a bowl, beat the butter until light and fluffy using an electric mixer. Beat in the egg, then stir in the curd cheese, followed by the sifted flour and baking powder, and salt. Cover the dough with cling film and set aside to rest for 1 hour in the fridge. Remove from the fridge 10 minutes before rolling, so that the dough is not too hard.

Sprinkle a little flour over a work surface and divide the dough into three equal portions, and roll each into 20 cm circles. Line a baking sheet with baking parchment and butter very lightly. Bake in middle rack of the oven for 25 minutes. Remove from the oven and transfer onto cooling racks until ready to use.

To make the filling, whisk the butter in a bowl using an electric mixer on a low speed until light and fluffy. Whisk in the Camembert. Now stir in the curd cheese, horseradish and sugar, and season with salt and pepper. Divide the mixture into two equal portions. In one half, stir in the parsley and the chopped ham.

Place the first disc on a tray and spread half the ham-based mixture over it. Place the second disc on top and spread the remaining half of the ham-based filling. Top with the final disc. Spread the plain mixture over the top and sides, just like you would ice a cake.

Crumble the pumpernickel between your fingers and sprinkle over the top of the torte. Not everyone likes pumpernickel, so leave it out if you prefer. Decorate to your heart's content with slices of salami, hard-boiled eggs, olives and radishes. Garnish with a few sprigs of curly parsley.

Palatschinken mit gesalzener Füllung

SAVOURY CRÊPES

MAKES 12

FOR THE CRÊPES

150 g plain flour

250 ml milk (or 125 ml milk and 125 ml double cream)

2 large eggs

2 large egg yolks

¼ tsp salt

4 tbsp butter, for frying

HERB FILLING (ENOUGH FOR 12 CRÊPES

150 g quark (or Austrian *Topfen* if available)

125 ml plain yoghurt

Pinch of salt, dried thyme and basil

200 g smoked ham, very finely chopped

Butter, for greasing

200 g tomatoes, skinned, deseeded and cut into small cubes

15 g grated Parmesan or other hard cheese of choice

Put the flour in a mixing bowl and slowly add the milk, then the whole eggs followed by the yolks and the salt, whisking with a balloon whisk between each addition, to a smooth thin batter. Melt a knob of butter in a medium-size frying pan over a medium to high heat, tilting the pan so that it is evenly coated in butter. Pour a small ladleful of batter into the pan and tilt quickly so that the batter thinly covers the surface of the pan and is evenly distributed. Cook for about a minute, or until the crêpe is light golden. Carefully flip over and cook on the other side (the other side will cook much more quickly).

Stack the crêpes on top of each other on a warmed plate and keep in a warm oven. Fill each pancake with your filling of choice.

In a bowl, mix the quark, yoghurt, salt, herbs and ham together. Spread each crêpe with the filling. Fold in half or like an envelope and place in a buttered ovenproof dish. Sprinkle over the cubed tomatoes and top with the Parmesan. Cook in a preheated 200°C/400°F/gas 6 oven for 10 to 15 minutes.

NOTE

The first crêpe is usually not a 'masterpiece' and should be eaten by the cook. By the time you come to make the second pancake, the pan will be at the optimum temperature and all subsequent pancakes will be just so.

MUSHROOM FILLING (ENOUGH FOR 12 CRÊPES)

20 g butter

½ medium onion, peeled and finely chopped

2 heaped tbsp finely chopped flat-leaf parsley

200 g button or fresh wild mushrooms, wiped clean and finely chopped

Salt and freshly ground pepper

1–2 tbsp crème fraîche (optional)

Melt the butter in a heavy-based frying pan over a medium to high heat until it begins to bubble. Fry the onion, until translucent, then add the parsley and the mushrooms. When all begins to bubble, reduce the heat to medium-low and cook until all the moisture has evaporated. Remove from the heat and season with salt and pepper. If using, add the crème fraîche gradually and make sure the filling isn't too runny.

Spread each crêpe with the filling, roll up, then place them in an ovenproof dish and keep them warm in a preheated 140°C/275°F/gas 1 oven, until they ready to serve. Alternatively, instead of rolling the crêpes, place the filling into the centre of each crêpe, then fold over like an envelope.

Lachsfleckerln

BAKED NOODLES WITH SALMON

SERVES 4

Butter, for greasing

1½ tbsp fine breadcrumbs

200 g extra-broad egg noodles
(or *Fleckerln* if available)

350 g poached deboned
salmon

70 g butter, at room
temperature

4 large eggs, separated

125 ml soured cream

Salt and freshly ground
pepper

Preheat to the oven to 180°C/350°F/gas 4.

Grease a 22 cm square baking dish with butter and sprinkle with the breadcrumbs, then tip out the excess breadcrumbs.

Break the noodles in half and boil in salted water for 7–10 minutes, until al dente, then drain. In the meantime, coarsely chop the salmon in a food processor and set aside.

In the bowl of an electric mixer, cream the butter until light and fluffy, then add in the egg yolks, one at a time, beating thoroughly after each addition. Stir in the soured cream and the salmon. Season with salt and pepper.

In a clean bowl, whisk the egg whites to stiff peaks.

Mix the noodles into the creamed mixture and fold in the egg whites. Transfer to the baking dish and bake for 35–40 minutes. Serve with a green salad.

NOTE
Square egg noodles (or *Fleckerln*) can be purchased in kosher shops or European delicatessens. Otherwise, standard egg noodles are a fine substitute.

Slawonischer Strudel

STRUDEL-LIKE BRIOCHE

SERVES 4

25 g fresh yeast

2 tsp sugar

250 ml lukewarm milk

500 g strong white flour,
plus extra for flouring

1½ tsp salt

3–4 egg yolks, depending
on size

100 g butter, melted

Sunflower oil, for greasing

150 g butter

**Note: All ingredients should
be at room temperature.**

YEAST EQUIVALENTS

1 tbsp/7 g of dry yeast
is equivalent to 15 g of
compressed or fresh
yeast. Dry yeast doesn't
dissolve well in milk, so
dissolve it in a little
warm water first, before
adding the milk called
for in the recipe.

In a warmed mixing bowl, cream the yeast with the sugar and add 5 tablespoons of the lukewarm milk until smooth. Move to a warm place to rise (either a sunny spot or an oven preheated to its lowest setting and then turned off) for 10–15 minutes, or until the mixture is half way up the bowl.

Sift the flour onto a clean work surface and add the salt. Make a large well in the centre and drop 3 egg yolks into the well. Add the raised yeast, drawing in the flour from the edges with your fingertips or a pastry scraper, and add the melted butter with the remainder of the milk. Gently work the dough until it is soft and slightly sticky: add another egg yolk if necessary

Knead the dough, scraping the work surface with the pastry scraper. Sprinkle a little extra flour around the dough so that it does not stick to the surface. Develop a rhythmic action and knead for between 10 and 15 minutes until soft and even-textured. The dough should be very elastic, soft and satiny-smooth.

Shape the dough into a ball. Place it into a warmed bowl lightly greased with oil, and turn the dough over so that it is evenly coated in oil. Cover with a damp tea towel and set aside to rise in a warm, draught-free place, for about 1–1½ hours.

When almost doubled in size, punch the dough down to its original size, then roll it out into a 30 x 40 cm rectangle.

Meanwhile beat the butter in a bowl using an electric mixer until light and fluffy. Spread the whipped butter over the dough, leaving a 2 cm clear border all round. Roll the rectangle into a cylinder, pressing down the seam to seal it.

Transfer the strudel onto a Swiss roll tray, seam-down. Press down the ends of the roll to seal. Cover with a dry tea towel and set aside to rise once again in a warm place, for 30–35 minutes, until almost doubled in size. Preheat oven to 200°C/400°F/gas 6. Bake for 25–35 minutes until golden in colour and hollow in sound when tapped on the surface. Serve with a green salad or a herring and potato salad.

Spinatroulade

SPINACH ROULADE

SERVES 4

FOR THE PASTRY

500 g spinach leaves

40 g butter, plus extra
for greasing

40 g plain flour

125 ml milk

Salt and freshly ground
pepper

4 large eggs, separated

FOR THE FILLING

1 tbsp butter

1 tbsp plain flour

125 ml milk

Salt

150 g ham, very finely
chopped

Grated Parmesan cheese,
to serve

AN INDULGENT
OPTION…
Tante Hertha used
to pour melted
butter over the
warm roulade.
Cholesterol wasn't
even in the picture
back then!

Preheat to the oven to 190°C/375°F/gas 5. Line a Swiss roll tray with baking parchment, then lightly grease it and dust it with flour.

Start by making the dough. Thoroughly wash the spinach, drain the excess water and cook in a covered pan on a gentle heat until wilted. Drain and when cool enough to handle, use your hands to squeeze out the remaining water. Purée the spinach in a food processor and set aside.

Melt the butter in a heavy-base saucepan. Whisk in the flour and cook until bubbling, for about a minute. Remove the pan from the heat and let it cool slightly, before gradually adding in the milk, whisking all the time. Return to the heat, bring to the boil, and whisk constantly until thick and the sauce comes away from the sides of the pan. Remove from the heat and season with salt and pepper. Mix in the spinach and transfer to a large bowl and set aside to cool, then fold the egg yolks into the mixture, one at a time.

In a separate clean bowl, whisk the egg whites into stiff peaks using an electric mixer. Using a spatula, gently fold the egg whites into the cooled spinach mixture. Spread the mixture evenly into the prepared baking tin and bake for 10–15 minutes, making sure a crust does not form, then remove from the oven.

Meanwhile, prepare the filling. In a saucepan, melt the butter over a medium heat, then add the flour, stirring all the while, until the mixture begins to bubble. Remove from the heat and while stirring vigorously with a wooden spoon, slowly add just enough milk to thicken. Return to the heat and continue to add the milk cautiously, stirring all the while, to prevent lumps from forming. The sauce should be of a medium thickness. Season with a little salt if necessary (the ham may be sufficiently salty). Simmer for another 2 minutes, then stir in the ham.

Carefully tip the pastry onto a clean tea towel, parchment side-up. Gently peel off the paper, then with the pastry still on the tea towel, roll and unroll the pastry twice (the pastry is pliable enough to do this without cracking) to 'train' it into shape. Spread the filling evenly over the surface using a spatula. Using the tea towel underneath to guide you, carefully roll the filled pastry as tightly as possible. Ease the roll onto a warmed serving dish, seam-side down. Sprinkle with Parmesan and serve immediately.

Beilagen, Salate und Gemüse

SIDES, SALADS AND VEGETABLES

The Naschmarkt is Vienna's central outdoor market established in the 16th century, where mainly bottled milk was sold. From 1793 onwards, all fruits and vegetables brought to Vienna by land had to be sold here, while goods arriving from the Danube were sold elsewhere. Ash (or *Asch*), from which milk bottles were made, led to the name Aschenmarkt. *Naschen* means 'to nibble or graze', so the evolvement of its name to Naschmarkt by 1820 seems very fitting.

A walk to the Naschmarkt from Hertha's centrally located flat took about 30 minutes. Hertha would have made her way down the fashionable Kärtner Straße, with its fine jewellers and exquisite boutiques, bypassing her beloved opera house and turning onto the Ring, its colourful red trams circling the inner city and beyond. Hertha's basket was filled almost daily with the fresh produce on offer – root vegetables, potatoes, cabbage for sauerkraut, cucumbers – all those most favoured in Viennese cuisine.

A standard *Beilage* (side dish) includes a type of bready dumpling. Usually accompanying a gravy-based meat dish, these dumplings are equally good on their own with a freshly made sauce and flavoured with parsley.

Erdäpfelkren

HORSERADISH MASH

SERVES 4

**500 g mashing potatoes
(such as Desiree or Romano)**

**100 g mayonnaise
(see page 68)**

85 ml lukewarm milk

1 tsp lemon juice

**Dash of tarragon vinegar
(optional)**

**2–3 tbsp finely grated
horseradish**

Salt

Boil the potatoes in their skins until tender. Drain and peel when cool enough to handle. Cut the potatoes into chunks and press them through a potato ricer into a mixing bowl.

Add the mayonnaise and milk in alternates one tablespoon at a time, until you achieve a creamy mash consistency. Add the lemon juice and a dash of vinegar, if using. Finally, add the horseradish and season with salt.

Perfect with grilled meat dishes or sausages.

Gebackenes Sauerkraut

BAKED SAUERKRAUT

SERVES 4

40 g streaky bacon

1 scant tablespoon sugar

1 medium small onion,
peeled and finely chopped

750 g sauerkraut, rinsed
and drained

Salt

1 kg floury potatoes

40 g lard or 40 ml sunflower
oil, plus extra lard for
greasing

150–200 g sausage of your
choice (Polish kielbassa, or
cured ham)

2 large eggs, hard-boiled
and sliced

125–150 ml soured cream

Preheat to the oven to 180°C/350°F/gas 4.

Cut the bacon into small cubes and gently fry it in its own fat until it begins to colour. Add the sugar and the onion and fry until the onion becomes translucent and is just starting to turn a golden colour.

Add the sauerkraut to the pan (the rinsing process can be omitted altogether – leave unrinsed for a tangier, slightly more acidic taste), season with a pinch of salt and cover. Turn up the heat until the contents come to the boil, then reduce to a simmer for 30 minutes, until the sauerkraut is tender. If the liquid looks like it is drying up, add a few teaspoons of water, but only add the water if absolutely necessary as it is best if the sauerkraut tenderises in its own juices.

Meanwhile, steam the potatoes in their skins until tender. When cooled, peel and thinly slice them. Fry the slices in the lard or oil with a pinch of salt to dry them out and get rid of any excess water.

Lightly grease a 22-cm square, 2.5-cm deep ovenproof dish. Slice the sausages or ham (or a combination of both). Cover the bottom of the dish with half the fried potatoes, then add a layer of sauerkraut, then a layer of sliced sausages or ham. Cover with the sliced eggs and the remainder of the potatoes. Top with the soured cream, making sure to cover entire surface. Bake uncovered for approximately 30–35 minutes. Serve with a mixed green salad.

Heringssalat

HERRING SALAD

SERVES 4

1.5 kg Jersey Royal or similar waxy potatoes

150 g carrots, peeled

150 g gherkins

150 g green beans

200–250 g herring in oil or Matjes herring fillets

1 tbsp capers, finely chopped

250 g Bramley apples, peeled and cubed

100 ml, or slightly less, olive oil

Dash of white wine vinegar

1 tsp Dijon mustard

125 ml soured cream

Salt and freshly ground pepper

Steam the potatoes in their skins with the whole carrots until tender. When cooled, peel the potatoes and cube them. Cut the carrots and gherkins into small cubes.

Boil the green beans for a couple of minutes until just tender. Drain and run under cold water, then slice them into 1 cm long pieces.

Rinse the herring thoroughly, pat with paper towels to remove the excess oil, and cut into small cubes into a bowl. Add the potatoes, carrots, gherkins, green beans, capers and apples.

In a separate bowl mix together the oil, vinegar, mustard and soured cream, then mix it into the herring mixture. Season with salt and pepper. Cover and marinate in the refrigerator for a few hours so that all the flavours infuse.

Remove from the refrigerator 30 minutes before serving. Serve on a mound of green lettuce, garnished with sliced hard-boiled eggs, miniature dill pickles, anchovies and 'rosettes' of homemade (see page 68) or shop-bought mayonnaise.

Kartoffelmayonnaisesalat

POTATO MAYONNAISE SALAD

SERVES 4

1.5 kg Fingerling, Jersey Royal or similar waxy potatoes

Salt

Vinegar water (6 tbsp water to 3 tsp light balsamic or mild white wine vinegar)

150 g homemade mayonnaise (see page 68)

Pinch of mild curry powder

40 g sweet gherkins, very finely cubed

1 tbsp capers, finely chopped

2 tsp chives, snipped (optional)

Dash of Tabasco sauce (optional)

Boil the potatoes in their skins until tender. When cooled, peel and thinly slice them, and sprinkle with salt. Transfer to a flat-bottomed dish.

Pour the vinegar water over the potato slices and marinate for no less than 1 hour, then drain any excess liquid.

In a separate bowl, mix the mayonnaise with the curry powder, gherkins, capers and, if using, the chives and Tabasco sauce. Now combine this mixture with the potatoes. Taste and adjust the seasoning and spices to your personal taste. Serve with Wiener Schnitzel (see page 61) or with any fish or grilled meat dishes.

Semmelknödeln

BREAD DUMPLINGS

SERVES 4

250 g stale white rolls or bread (in Austria you can find bread specifically for dumplings called *Knödel Brot*)

1 large egg

1 large egg yolk

200 ml milk

20 g butter

1 medium onion, finely chopped

1 heaped tbsp chopped flat-leaf parsley

1 tsp salt

2–4 tbsp plain flour, plus 4 tbsp for the coating

Cube the rolls or bread to the size of croutons and place into a large bowl. In a separate bowl, beat the egg and the egg yolk with the milk and pour over the cubed bread, gently stirring with a wooden spoon to make sure all the cubes are coated with the egg mixture.

Meanwhile, heat the butter in a heavy-base frying pan over a medium to high heat until it begins to bubble. Add the onion and fry until translucent. Add the parsley and fry a little longer, making sure that it does not become crisp. Remove from the heat and pour over the cubed bread. Season with the salt and mix together with the wooden spoon, gently packing down the bread in the bowl so that it soaks up all the flavours. Set aside to absorb the liquid for 10–15 minutes. During this time, gently turn the mixture over with the spoon a couple of times, pack down again and leave to rest.

After this period, the mixture should be moist, but not dripping wet. Add 2 tablespoons of the flour, mixing it in with the wooden spoon. Feel the texture with your fingers, and if the mass holds together with a little pressure, then no more flour is needed; otherwise add 1–2 more tablespoonfuls.

Keep a bowl of warm water to hand. In another shallow medium-size bowl, sieve 4 tablespoons of flour for the 'coating'. Wet one hand and scoop out a ball of mixture, about the size of a peach. Roll into a firm ball, firmly pressing the mixture together so that it holds its shape. Repeat until all the mixture is used. Roll each dumpling in the sifted flour to just coat it and set aside on a plate.

Bring a large pan of salted water to the boil. Carefully lower the dumplings in batches into the pan and boil, uncovered, for 2 minutes, then reduce the heat and simmer very gently for another 15 minutes. Use a slotted spoon to gently lift them from the pot, draining off all the water and place onto a warm plate. Keep the batches warm in a low oven.

Serve immediately with goulash or a meat dish. Any leftovers can be sliced and fried in a little butter and served as an accompaniment to salads, meat or vegetable dishes.

Warmer Krautsalat

WARM CABBAGE SALAD

SERVES 4

500 g white cabbage

6 tbsp white wine vinegar

1 tsp salt

1 tsp sugar

1 tsp caraway seeds

100 g speck (cured fatty bacon), cut into 0.5 cm cubes

Remove the outer leaves of the cabbage and discard. Finely shred the rest of the cabbage using a mandolin if you have one, if not a sharp knife will do – mind your fingers!

Place the shredded cabbage in a large bowl. Pour boiling water over the top and let stand a few minutes. Drain and repeat the process twice more, draining well between each scalding.

In a saucepan, mix the vinegar, salt, sugar and caraway seeds with 3 tablespoons of water and bring to the boil. Pour over the well-drained cabbage. Cover with a plate or lid to fit the bowl and allow to stand for 30 minutes.

Drain the liquid into a saucepan and bring to the boil. Remove from the heat and pour over the cabbage.

Gently fry the speck until crisp but not too browned. Remove from the heat, lifting it out with a slotted spoon, and drain on a paper towel. Transfer the cabbage onto a warmed serving dish and just before serving, sprinkle the warm bacon bits on top. Serve with roast pork or sausages.

Kürbisgemüse

CREAMED PUMPKIN

SERVES 4

600 g pumpkin

1 tsp salt

40 g lard (or 20 ml sunflower oil and 20 g butter)

½ small onion, peeled and very finely chopped

1 tsp paprika

1 tbsp white wine vinegar

1 tbsp tomato purée

1 tsp caraway seeds

125 ml soured cream

1 tsp plain flour

Freshly ground pepper

Peel and seed the pumpkin and coarsely grate or shred in a food processor. Transfer to a mixing bowl and stir in the salt. Cover with cling film and set aside for no less than 1 hour. Drain.

Heat the lard (or oil and butter) in a stainless steel saucepan and fry the onion on a medium heat until light golden. Stir in the paprika and immediately remove the pan from the heat (paprika should not be allowed to fry for any length of time because it turns bitter). Add the vinegar and return the pan to the heat. Add the drained pumpkin together with the tomato purée and the caraway seeds. Don't be tempted to add any fluids – the pumpkin will yield enough of its own juice. Mix well and cover. Bring to a rolling boil and then immediately reduce the heat and simmer for 35–40 minutes, until the pumpkin is tender. Stir a couple of times during cooking time to prevent the mixture sticking to the bottom of the pan.

Meanwhile, mix the soured cream with the flour in a bowl. Once the pumpkin is tender, stir in the soured cream/flour mixture and gently bring it back to a gentle simmer, covered, for another 10 minutes, making sure that the heat is not too high. Adjust the seasoning if necessary and add a few grindings of pepper.

The flavour of this dish improves with time so can be eaten up to two days after cooking. Serve with roast pork or chicken.

Serviettenknödel

DUMPLING STEAMED IN A NAPKIN

SERVES 4

FOR THE DUMPLING

320 g day-old white rolls
or variety of white bread

2 large eggs

2 large egg yolks

500 ml milk

100 g speck (cured fatty
bacon), cut into 0.5 cm
cubes

3 tbsp finely chopped
flat-leaf parsley

1 tsp salt

6–8 tbsp breadcrumbs

FOR THE TOPPING

20 g butter

20 g fine breadcrumbs

Cut the rolls or bread into 1 cm cubes. Place in a large bowl.

In a separate bowl, lightly beat the eggs and yolks with the milk and pour over the cubed bread. Cover and soak for 30 minutes.

Have a tea towel ready, which has been wrung out in cold water and lightly buttered on one side. Bring a large pan of salted water to the boil.

Fry the speck in its own fat on a very low heat until it begins to just colour. Remove from the heat and pour over the soaked bread. Using a large wooden spoon, stir in the parsley, salt and breadcrumbs. Then use your hands to gather the mixture into one large dumpling, and place it in the centre of the buttered tea towel. Gather the four corners and tie them together firmly so that the knot does not unravel, but make sure the dumpling has enough space to expand while it cooks.

Slot the handle of a long-handled wooden spoon through the ends of the napkin and gently lower the 'parcel' into the pan, resting the handle along the edge of the pan so that the dumpling does not touch the bottom. Loosely cover the pan with a lid. Once the water has come to a boil again, reduce the heat and simmer gently for 45 minutes to 1 hour.

Before the hour is up, prepare the breadcrumb topping. Melt the butter in a frying pan on a medium to high heat until it begins to bubble. Add the breadcrumbs and stir them in the butter until they are pale golden and a little crisp.

When the dumpling is cooked, take the pan off the heat and carefully lift the dumpling from pan. When cool enough to handle, remove the dumpling from the tea towel and transfer to a warmed plate. Sprinkle the fried breadcrumbs on top and cut into thick slices. Alternatively, it can be 'torn' into to small pieces shortly before being served and sprinkled with fried breadcrumbs.

Bäckereien

BISCUITS AND COOKIES

Most of the biscuits in this chapter are traditionally made for the Christmas season. Gingerbread, meringues and chocolate truffles are hung on beautifully adorned trees on Christmas Eve. The truffles are wrapped in delicate tissue paper in the colour that complements the overall decor. Red, for instance, flatters the more traditional style of tree, whereas white creates a more elegant look for gold and silver Christmas ornaments. And then there are the pastels to choose from... These tissues are either bought pre-cut to size or large sheets of paper are cut by children under the supervision of their mothers or grandmothers.

More than in any other section of Hertha's book, many names are affiliated with these recipes – aunts, cousins and friends who would have, fittingly for the season being honoured, shared their favourite recipes and made them timeless.

Having tested all of these delicacies again when writing the book, we came to the realisation that it seems a shame to enjoy them for such a short season. Chocolate-laden recipes are welcome all year round, and the variety of thin wafers can be served in the summer months with ice creams and jellies. One biscuit, however, is sacred to the Christmas season: the *Vanillekipferl* (see page 136), a melt-in-your-mouth shortbread in the shape of a half-moon dusted with homemade vanilla sugar (see page 136): they should truly remain a rarefied treat.

Butterbrötchen

BREAD-AND-BUTTER SANDWICH BISCUITS

MAKES 24

FOR THE BISCUITS

200 g plain flour

120 g caster sugar

120 g unsalted butter

40 g dark (70% cocoa) chocolate, finely grated

30 g ground hazelnuts

1 large egg

FOR THE GLAZE

100 g icing sugar

2 large egg yolks

Preheat the oven to 150°C/300°F/gas 2.

Start by making the biscuits. Sift the flour onto a clean work surface and mix in the sugar. Chop the butter into small cubes and use your fingertips to work it into the flour and sugar, until you reach a crumbly consistency. Alternatively put the flour, sugar and diced butter in a food processor and process until the mixture resembles fine breadcrumbs.

Add the grated chocolate, hazelnuts and egg, and mix very quickly to form a dough. Divide the dough in half and roll it out into two logs about 5 cm in diameter. Wrap each log in cling film and refrigerate for 1 hour.

Remove from the refrigerator and cut into 5-mm thick slices. Place the rounds on a baking sheet lined with baking parchment and bake for 30–35 minutes.

Remove from the oven and transfer the biscuits onto wire racks to cool.

In the meantime, make the glaze. In a bowl, whisk the icing sugar with the egg yolks until smooth. Once cooled, spread each biscuit thinly with the glaze, as you would butter a slice of bread. Store in airtight containers for a few days or in the freezer for up to three months.

Damenperletten

RAISIN SHORTCAKES

MAKES 38

120 g sultanas

3 tbsp rum

120 g plain flour

120 g unsalted butter,
at room temperature

120 g icing sugar

2 large egg yolks

1 tsp homemade vanilla
sugar (see page 136), or
½ tsp vanilla extract

30 g lightly toasted almonds,
roughly chopped

In a small bowl, soak the sultanas in the rum for 2–3 hours.

Preheat the oven to 190°C/375°F/gas 5 and line a baking sheet with baking parchment.

Sift the flour into a bowl. In a separate bowl, cream the butter until it is light, then whisk in the sugar until light and fluffy. Beat in one egg yolk at a time, then add the vanilla.

Using a wooden spoon, gently fold the sifted flour into the mixture, along with the soaked sultanas until incorporated.

Drop one teaspoon of the batter for each biscuit, spacing them well apart. Flatten the biscuits with a fork dipped in cold water, and sprinkle with the chopped almonds.

Bake in batches for 20–25 minutes, until golden brown and crisp around the edges. Leave the biscuits to cool on the baking sheet for about 10 minutes before peeling them off the baking parchment and transferring them onto cooling racks. Allow to cool completely before storing in airtight containers for up to two weeks. Not suitable for freezing.

Gefüllte Lebkuchen

FILLED GINGERBREAD

MAKES 24

FOR THE BISCUITS

90 ml runny honey

60 g granulated sugar

½ tsp ground cinnamon

Pinch of ground cloves

Pinch of ground nutmeg

40 g butter, melted and cooled

250 g plain flour

½ tsp baking powder

1 large egg

FOR THE FILLING

60 g ground hazelnuts

60 g icing sugar

30 g mixed peel, finely chopped

1 large egg

20 g blanched almonds, halved, to garnish (see page 108)

1 egg white, for brushing

Start by making the biscuits. Heat the honey in a pan over a medium heat, then add the sugar and spices, stirring all the while for about 5 to 7 minutes, until the sugar has dissolved (be careful the honey does not come to a boil). Remove from the heat and set aside to cool.

In a separate pan, only just melt the butter over a medium heat, then set aside to cool.

Sieve the flour with the baking powder into a large bowl, pour in the cooled honey/spice mixture and the cooled melted butter, the egg, and mix with a large wooden spoon to form a soft dough. Transfer into a smaller bowl and cover with cling film. Refrigerate overnight.

The following day, mix all the ingredients for the filling in a bowl.

Preheat the oven to 180°C/350°F/gas 4. Line a baking sheet with baking parchment.

Take the dough out of the refrigerator and set aside for 15 minutes before rolling out half the dough on a clean, floured work surface. Return the other half of dough to the refrigerator.

With a floured rolling pin, roll out the dough to a thickness of 5 mm. Using a cookie cutter, cut into 6-cm circles.

Place ½ teaspoon of the filling into the centre of every other circle and cover with a plain circle, pressing down the edges to seal. Transfer the rounds to a baking sheet lined with baking parchment, setting each round 2 cm apart. Brush the tops with egg white and place half an almond in the centre of each biscuit, pressing down gently. Bake for 20 minutes, to a deep golden brown colour. Remove from the oven, peel the biscuits off the baking parchment and cool on wire racks.

Incorporate any left-over dough into the remaining half of the refrigerated dough and repeat the procedure, until all the dough has been used.

Once the biscuits have cooled completely, store in airtight containers. They will keep for several weeks in a cool, dark place.

Grazer Zwieback

GRAZ RUSKS

MAKES 22 SLICES

5 large egg whites

85 g icing sugar

75 g plain flour, plus extra for
dusting

Grated zest of ½ lemon

25 g unsalted butter, melted
and cooled

Butter, for greasing

80 g icing sugar mixed with
1 tsp homemade vanilla sugar
(see page 136), for
coating/dusting

Preheat the oven to 160°C/325°F/gas 3.

In the bowl of an electric mixer, whisk the egg whites to soft peaks. Gradually add two-thirds of the icing sugar, and whisk on a high speed until very stiff. Using a large metal spoon, fold in the remaining icing sugar, along with the flour and grated lemon zest. Finally, carefully stir in the melted and cooled butter.

Grease and flour a 500-g loaf tin. Transfer the mixture into the tin and bake for 45–50 minutes, until golden brown. Remove from the oven and turn onto a wire rack to cool. Because it is such an airy cake, ideally, it should be left to rest overnight. This helps it solidify and make it easier to cut.

The following day, preheat oven to 150°C/300°F/gas 2.

Using a serrated knife, thinly slice the loaf into 6-mm thin slices. Coat both sides of each slice in the vanilla sugar and place on a baking sheet. Place in the oven for 20–25 minutes until golden brown, then turn over the slices and bake for a further 8–10 minutes. Remove from the oven and if you wish, dust lightly once more with vanilla sugar. Allow to cool completely before storing in airtight containers for up to three weeks. Not suitable for freezing.

Husarenkrapferln

THUMBPRINT BISCUITS

MAKES 38

210 g plain flour, plus extra

70 g caster sugar

140 g cold unsalted butter, diced

2 large egg yolks

1 large egg white

30 g blanched almonds, coarsely chopped

30 g granulated sugar

100 g apricot or raspberry jam

Sift the flour into a food processor and add the caster sugar and diced butter. Process until the mixture resembles coarse breadcrumbs. Turn out onto a clean work surface and make a well in the centre. Add the egg yolks and mix together, using a metal spatula to draw in the flour. Press the dough into a ball, wrap it in cling film and refrigerate for 30 minutes to 1 hour until firm.

Preheat oven to 160°C/325°F/gas 3. Line a baking sheet with baking parchment.

Remove the dough from the refrigerator and form small 2.5-cm balls. Space them 2.5 cm apart on the baking sheet.

Tip a little flour into a small bowl. Dip the end of a wooden spoon into the flour and gently press the underside of the spoon into each ball, leaving a deep indentation in the centre of each biscuit.

Brush a little egg white over each biscuit and sprinkle with the almonds and the granulated sugar. Some of the topping will inevitably end up on the baking sheet, but these sugary crumbs are delicious once cooked! Bake for 20–25 minutes, until golden brown. Remove from the oven and transfer the biscuits onto cooling racks.

In a saucepan over a low heat, warm the jam to make it more spreadable and then let it cool. Once the biscuits have cooled, spoon a little jam into each centre. Allow the jam centres to cool completely (the jam will turn hard) before storing. Place a sheet of wax paper between each biscuit for storage purposes. Store in airtight containers for up to one week or in the freezer for up to three months.

BLANCHING ALMONDS

If you are blanching your own almonds, drop the unpeeled almonds into a pan of boiling water. Cover and immediately remove from the heat. Allow to stand for 5 minutes, then drain and peel while still fairly hot. Pinch the end of each almond between your thumb and index finger – the skins will slide off effortlessly.

Honig-Butterkeks Mini

MINI'S HONEY BUTTER BISCUITS

MAKES 20–22

FOR THE DOUGH

280 g plain flour

100 g icing sugar

200 g unsalted butter,
at room temperature, plus
extra for greasing

1 large egg

1 tsp homemade vanilla
sugar (see page 136), or
½ tsp vanilla extract

Pinch of salt

1 large egg white

FOR THE FILLING

100 g runny honey

6 walnuts, chopped

100 g mixed peel, very finely
chopped

1 large egg yolk

Start by making the biscuits. Sift the flour into a food processor and add the remaining dough ingredients, except the egg white. Process until all the ingredients have been incorporated.

Transfer the mixture onto a floured surface and knead into a dough. Form into a ball, wrap in cling film and refrigerate for two hours.

Roll out the dough to a thickness of 3 mm and cut out 5-cm rounds with a cookie cutter. Using an apple corer, stamp out the centre of every other biscuit. There are special cookie cutters which are designed with a hole in the centre but this method works just as well.

In a small bowl, lightly whisk the egg white with a fork. Brush each of the solid rounds with egg white and place a holed round on top. Place on a buttered baking sheet and refrigerate while making the filling. Preheat oven to 200°C/400°F/gas 6.

To prepare the filling, gently bring the honey to the boil in a saucepan, stirring occasionally. Add the nuts and mixed peel, and cook for a further 2 minutes, stirring continuously. Remove from the heat and set aside to cool, stirring occasionally.

Remove the biscuits from refrigerator and with a teaspoon, carefully place some of the filling into the hole of each biscuit, being careful not to spill any onto the rim. Brush the rim with egg yolk and bake for 6–8 minutes until golden brown. Store in airtight containers for up to one week or in the freezer for up to three months.

Ischler Törtchen

ISCHLER TARTLETS

MAKES 20

250 g plain flour

140 g unsalted butter

80 g caster sugar

40 g ground almonds

1 large egg yolk

1 tbsp milk

40 g icing sugar

100 g apricot or redcurrant jam

Preheat the oven to 180°C/350°F/gas 4.

Make sure all ingredients are cold. For this purpose, measure the flour into a metal bowl and refrigerate for 1 hour.

Sieve the flour into a food processor and add the diced butter. Process until the mixture resembles coarse breadcrumbs. Add the sugar and ground almonds and mix again. Tip the mixture onto a clean work surface and make a well in the centre. In a bowl, beat the egg yolk with the milk and then pour into the centre of the flour mixture. Mix, first with a knife and then with your hands until the dough holds together. Form the dough into a flat disc and divide it into two equal portions. Refrigerate half the dough.

Roll out the other half of the dough to a thickness of 3 mm and cut out 6-cm rounds with a scalloped cookie cutter. Cut a hole in the centre of every other biscuit using an apple corer. Gather any scraps of dough and form them into a ball, then flatten into a disk. Wrap in cling film and refrigerate until ready to use.

Gently transfer the biscuits onto an ungreased baking sheet, leaving about 2.5 cm between each biscuit. Bake for 12–15 minutes, until the edges start to colour.

Remove from the oven and allow to cool on the baking sheet for about a minute, then transfer the biscuits onto cooling racks to cool completely.

While the first batch of biscuits is cooling, use up the remaining dough and the saved scraps in the same way.

Once the biscuits have cooled, dust only those biscuits with the hole in the centre with icing sugar. In a saucepan, warm the jam on a low heat to make it more spreadable, then set aside to cool slightly. Sandwich the jam between the solid biscuits and the dusted ones. Store in airtight containers for up to one week or in the freezer for up to three months.

Ischli Fank

SPICED BISCUITS

MAKES 46

FOR THE BISCUITS

280 g unsalted butter,
at room temperature

140 g caster sugar

1 large egg

½ tsp ground cinnamon

½ tsp ground cloves

1 scant tsp lemon zest

280 g plain flour

140 g ground almonds

125 ml set honey

**FOR THE CHOCOLATE
GLAZE**

100 g plain (50% cocoa)
chocolate, for glazing

Start by making the biscuits. In the bowl of an electric mixer, cream the butter with the sugar until light and fluffy. Beat in the egg until it has been incorporated. Stir in the spices and the lemon zest.

Sift the flour into a large bowl and stir in the ground almonds, followed by the creamed butter, mixing all together. Cover with cling film and refrigerate for 45 minutes. Remove the dough from the fridge and divide it into three equal portions. Roll each portion into a 4-cm wide sausage, then wrap each roll in waxed paper and refrigerate for 30–40 minutes.

Preheat the oven to 180°C/350°F/gas 4.

Cut the rolls into 6-mm thick rounds. Place them on a baking sheet lined with baking parchment, leaving a little space between slices and bake for approximately 25 minutes until golden brown, then remove from oven. Once cooled, sandwich two biscuits together with a little honey.

To make the chocolate glaze, break the chocolate into small pieces and place in a heatproof bowl. Melt the chocolate, either by heating in a microwave for 20–30 seconds or by placing in the centre of an oven preheated to 100°C/200°F/gas¼ until it has melted to a silky smooth texture, about 10–15 minutes. Remove, stir until smooth and allow to cool slightly before spreading a thin layer over the top of each biscuit.

Allow the biscuits to cool. Store in airtight containers for up to one week or in the freezer for up to three months, placing a sheet of waxed paper between each layer of biscuits.

Lebkuchen Gertraud Dergans

GINGERBREAD GERTRAUD

MAKES 40

250 g dark, runny honey

125 g granulated sugar

1 tsp ground cloves

3 tbsp ground cinnamon

1 tsp allspice

80 g unsalted butter

60 g candied lemon peel

30 g candied orange peel

30 g almonds

125 g hazelnuts

3 large eggs

500 g plain flour

1 tsp baking soda dissolved in 1 tbsp water

Mix the honey and sugar in a pan. Place over a medium heat and bring to a gentle boil, stirring regularly, until the sugar has dissolved. Remove from the heat and mix in the ground cloves, cinnamon and allspice. Set aside to cool.

In a separate pan, melt the butter and set aside to cool. Using a sharp knife, very finely chop the candied lemon and orange peel, almonds and hazelnuts (this can be done in a food processor if you prefer).

In a small bowl, beat two of the eggs until frothy. In a large bowl, sift the flour and add the melted butter mixture, the beaten eggs and the dissolved baking soda. Mix with a wooden spoon to incorporate all the ingredients. Use your hands to shape the mixture into a flat disc. Place the dough in a small bowl, cover with cling film and refrigerate overnight.

The following day, preheat the oven to 160°C/325°F/gas 3. Line a baking sheet with baking parchment.

Roll out the dough to a thickness of 5 mm and cut out with a 5-cm round cookie cutter. Place the biscuits on the prepared baking sheet and brush with the remaining egg, lightly beaten. Bake on the middle rack of the oven for 20–25 minutes until golden brown. Store in airtight containers for up to four weeks or in the freezer for up to three months.

Linzerli

ALMOND RINGS

MAKES 36

200 g plain flour, plus extra for dusting

1½ tsp cocoa powder

¾ tsp ground cinnamon

125 g caster sugar

125 g unsalted butter, cold, plus extra for greasing

1 large egg, lightly beaten

125 g ground almonds

Grated zest of ½ lemon

100 g raspberry jam (or runny honey)

1 large egg yolk, for brushing

Icing sugar, for dusting

Preheat the oven to 180°C/350°F/gas 4. Line a baking sheet with baking parchment.

Sift the flour into a food processor and add the cocoa powder, cinnamon and sugar. Cut the butter into dice and add to the flour. Process briefly until the mixture reseembles fine breadcrumbs. Add the ground almonds and lemon zest and process for a further 10 seconds.

Tip the mixture out onto a clean work surface and make a well in the centre. Pour in the beaten eggs and mix quickly, first wiht the tip of a knife and then with your hands. Work into a fairly firm dough, adding more flour if necessary.

Roll out the dough to a 5-mm thickness. Cut the dough into rounds using a 5-cm round cookie cutter. Cut a hole in the centre of every other biscuit using an apple corer. Brush the whole rounds with either warmed and then cooled raspberry jam or honey. Use sparingly so that the jam doesn't bubble over during baking. Place a perforated biscuit on top of each solid biscuit. Lightly brush the tops of each biscuit with egg yolk and place in the preheated oven. Bake for 25–30 minutes, watching in case they are ready a little earlier. If filled with raspberry jam dust with icing sugar. If filled with honey, leave plain. Store in airtight containers for up to one week or in the freezer for up to three months.

Parmesan-Stangerln

PARMESAN STICKS

MAKES 28

200 g plain flour

140 g butter, cold

1 tsp salt

3 tbsp soured cream

1 egg yolk

Grated Parmesan cheese,
for sprinkling

Chill the flour in a bowl in the refrigerator for 30 minutes. Sieve the cold flour into a food processor and add the butter, diced. Process until the mixture resembles coarse breadcrumbs. Tip out onto a clean work surface, sprinkle over the salt, add the soured cream, and using the blade of a knife initially and then your hands, quickly bring the mixture into a ball. Divide the ball in two and shape each into a 5-cm thick log. Place each on a plate, cover with cling film and refrigerate for 30 minutes.

Preheat the oven to 220°C/425°F/gas 7. Line a baking sheet with baking parchment.

Take out one half of the dough from the refrigerator. Cut off small pieces of dough the size of a walnut and roll between your hands into 10-cm lengths. Place on the baking sheet and brush each with the egg yolk and sprinkle the grated Parmesan cheese liberally on top. Bake for 15 minutes to a rich golden colour. Cheese can burn quickly, so do watch the sticks! Test one before removing the entire sheet. When done, transfer onto wire racks to cool. Repeat with the other half.

The sticks taste best while still warm and are delicious served for tea or with a salad.

Pfeffernüssli Elisabeth Gulacsy

ELISABETH GULACSY'S ALLSPICE BISCUITS

MAKES 46

250 g caster sugar

2 large eggs, at room temperature

¾ tsp ground nutmeg

½ tsp ground cinnamon

¼ tsp ground cloves

75 g mixed peel, very finely chopped

125 g ground almonds

250 g plain flour, plus extra for dusting

Butter, for greasing

Mix all ingredients, except for the flour, in a large bowl or food processor. Gradually add the flour and knead or process to form a dough. (If you prefer slightly higher biscuits, add a pinch of baking powder to the flour.) Roll out dough on a clean, lightly floured work surface to a thickness of 1 cm. Cut out 5-cm rounds using a cookie cutter.

Lightly grease a baking sheet. Place the rounds on the baking sheet and set aside to rest overnight in a warm place.

The following day, preheat the oven to 150°C/300°F/gas 2. Just before baking, turn the biscuits over on the baking sheet and bake for approximately 30 minutes. Store in airtight containers for up to one week or in the freezer for up to three months.

Rumovè Kuličky

RUM BALLS

MAKES 68

240 g dark (70% cocoa) chocolate

280 g ground walnuts

360 g icing sugar

8 tbsp dark rum

Granulated sugar, for coating

Break the chocolate into pieces and place in a heatproof bowl. Melt the chocolate, either by heating in a microwave for 20–30 seconds or by placing the bowl over a pan of just simmering water. Make sure the bowl is not touching the water and monitor carefully. Alternatively you can melt the chocolate the way Hertha would have (see Note below). Stir the chocolate until smooth and set aside to cool.

In a separate bowl, mix the ground walnuts, icing sugar and rum together, and stir in the cooled chocolate. Gather into a large ball. Take a heaped teaspoon of the mixture and roll it between the palms of your hands to form 2.5-cm balls.

Pour the sugar into a shallow bowl and roll the rum balls in it until evenly coated. Place on a baking tray, cover with a sheet of wax paper and leave to set for several hours or overnight. Store in airtight container for up to two weeks. Not suitable for freezing.

NOTE
Put the chocolate pieces in an ovenproof bowl and place in the centre of an oven preheated to 100°C/200°F/gas ¼ until it has just melted to a silky smooth texture, about 10–15 minutes. Be sure to monitor the chocolate so that it does not burn. Remove from the oven, stir until smooth and set aside to cool.

Schokoladenkugeln

CHOCOLATE TRUFFLES

MAKES 20 TRUFFLES

200 g dark (70% cocoa) chocolate

4 heaped tbsp of a mix of walnuts and coarsely chopped praline (see page 200) (optional)

50 g unsalted butter

50 g icing sugar

1 large egg, at room temperature

4 tbsp chocolate vermicelli (or 4 tbsp cocoa powder mixed with 1 tsp icing sugar)

Break the chocolate into small pieces and place in a heatproof bowl. Melt the chocolate, either by heating in a microwave for 20–30 seconds or by placing the bowl over a pan of just simmering water. Make sure the bowl is not touching the water and monitor carefully. Alternatively you can melt the chocolate the way Hertha would have done (see Note on page 122). Stir the chocolate until smooth and set aside to cool.

Pulse the nut mixture to a fine texture, but not so fine that it becomes a paste. Set aside.

In the (warmed) bowl of an electric mixer, cream the butter until it turns light in colour. Beat in the icing sugar, then the egg and continue to beat until all is incorporated. Add the cooled chocolate, beating all the while.

Using a wooden spoon, stir in the pulsed nuts. Refrigerate, uncovered, for a 1–1½ hours to firm up enough to make the rolling process possible.

Take a heaped teaspoon of the mixture and roll it between the palms of your hands to form 2.5-cm balls.

Pour the chocolate vermicelli and/or the cocoa powder into separate shallow bowls and roll the balls in the coating until evenly coated. Place on a baking tray, cover with a sheet of wax paper and leave to set for several hours or overnight. Store in airtight containers for up to two weeks. Not suitable for freezing.

Schokoladentaferln mit Zitroneneis

CHOCOLATE WAFERS WITH LEMON GLAZE

MAKES 15–20

FOR THE BISCUITS

500 g plain flour

70 g unsalted butter, diced

140 g caster sugar

140 g dark (70% cocoa)
chocolate, grated

1 large egg yolk

85 ml single cream

FOR THE LEMON GLAZE

250 g icing sugar

Juice of at least 1 lemon

Start by making the biscuits. Sift the flour into a food processor and add the butter. Process until the mixture resembles coarse breadcrumbs. Add the sugar and grated chocolate and process briefly to mix through and then tip the mixture out onto a clean surface.

In a separate bowl, combine the egg yolk and cream. Make a well in centre of the flour mixture and pour in almost all the egg/cream liquid (reserve just a little for later). Using the tip of a knife, start mixing in the liquid, then use your hands to quickly knead into a fairly stiff dough. If the dough looks too stiff, add the remaining cream (the dough should be fairly stiff but still rollable).

Preheat the oven to 180°C/350°F/gas 4.

Lightly flour a clean work surface, then roll out the dough to a 1-cm thickness. Cut into 6 x 2.5-cm rectangles.

Line a baking tray with baking parchment. Transfer the rectangles onto the tray and bake for 15–20 minutes. Check after 15 minutes to make sure that the wafers are not burning. Remove from the oven and place on wire racks to cool.

To make the lemon glaze, sieve the icing sugar into a bowl. Gradually add the lemon juice, 1 teaspoon to start off with, then almost drop by drop, stirring in between each addition to make sure the glaze doesn't get too runny. The glaze should be of a spreadable consistency.

Spread each wafer with the glaze. Set aside until the glaze hardens, then store in airtight containers for up to two weeks or in the freezer for up to three months.

Schokoladenkugeln Mini

MINI'S CHOCOLATE BALLS

MAKES 52

2 large eggs

200 g caster sugar

250 g whole unpeeled almonds, ground

125 g dark (70% cocoa) chocolate, grated

1 tsp ground cinnamon

2 tbsp plain flour

Icing sugar, for coating

Whisk the eggs with sugar until the mixture is a very pale colour. Stir in the remaining ingredients (minus the icing sugar). It is important that the mixing be done very quickly so that the mixture holds together.

Form 2.5-cm balls in the palms of your hands. Pour the icing sugar into a shallow bowl and roll the balls in it until evenly coated.

Place on a well-greased baking tray to set for several hours, but not overnight.

When the balls have set, preheat the oven to 150°C/300°F/gas 2. Bake for 25–30 minutes. As they bake, they expand and crack open – don't worry, this is all part of the process and does not compromise the delicious flavour! Store in airtight containers for up to one week or in the freezer for up to three months.

Schokoplätzchen

CHOCOLATE DROPS

MAKES 25

50 g dark (70% cocoa) chocolate

70 g unsalted butter

100 g icing sugar

70 g ground almonds

Preheat the oven to 140°C/275°F/gas 1.

Break the chocolate into small pieces and place in a heatproof bowl. Melt the chocolate, either by heating in a microwave for 20–30 seconds or by placing the bowl of a pan of just simmering water. Make sure the bowl is not touching the water and monitor carefully. Alternatively you can melt the chocolate the way Hertha would have done (see Note on page 122). Stir the chocolate until smooth and set aside to cool.

Line a baking sheet with baking parchment. In the bowl of an electric mixer, beat the butter until light and fluffy. Stir in the icing sugar and then the cooled chocolate. Finally stir in the ground almonds.

Drop a teaspoon of the mixture onto the prepared baking sheet (but do not flatten!). Space the drops about 3 cm apart as they will expand.

Bake for 55–60 minutes. As there is no real way of testing them to see if they are ready, keep a watch around the 50-minute mark to make sure they are not burning. Remove from the oven and transfer onto wire racks to cool. Store in airtight containers for up to two weeks or in the freezer for up to three months.

Spanischer Wind

MERINGUES

**MAKES 25 LARGE OR
50 SMALL MERINGUES**

3 large egg whites,
at room temperature

180 g caster sugar

Preheat the oven to 120°C/250°F/gas ½. Line a baking sheet with baking parchment.

In the bowl of an electric mixer, beat the egg whites to stiff peaks. Gradually add one-third of the sugar, one tablespoon at the time, whisking all the while (this should take about 10 minutes). Carefully fold in the remaining sugar using a large metal spoon. The mixture will be stiff, silky-smooth and glossy.

If you are making large meringues, drop a heaped tablespoon of the egg white onto the prepared baking sheet. If you prefer smaller meringues, use a heaped teaspoon. Meringues don't expand, so there is no need to space them too far apart. Bake on the bottom shelf of the oven for between 1½ and 2 hours (depending on size) until the meringues are firm with a hint of colour. Turn the oven off but leave the meringues in the oven with the door closed to cool for another few hours or even overnight so that they dry out slowly. Store in airtight containers for several days. Not suitable for freezing.

NOTE
The small meringues were hung on the tree at Christmas time. You would place a short piece of cotton thread in a U-shape on the baking sheet and drop a teaspoon of egg white mixture at the open ends, to seal them. When baked, you have built-in loops ready for hanging on the tree like beautiful drops of snow!

Weihnachtslebkuchen Tante Fränzchen

AUNT FRÄNZCHEN'S CHRISTMAS GINGERBREAD

MAKES 88

FOR THE GINGERBREAD

250 ml icing sugar

1 tsp baking soda

1 tsp ground cinnamon

1 tsp allspice

1 tsp ground cloves

500 g plain flour, plus an extra 100 g if needed

250 ml runny honey

1 large egg, lightly beaten

FOR THE LEMON GLAZE

250 g icing sugar

Juice of at least 1 lemon

Start by making the gingerbread. Line a baking sheet with baking parchment.

Sift all the dry ingredients onto a clean work surface (use only 500 g of flour for now). Add the honey and the lightly beaten egg and knead into a pliable dough. If the dough feels a little wet and sticky, add a little more flour. Form the dough into a ball, patting it down to flatten it a little, then cover with cling film and refrigerate overnight.

The following day, preheat the oven to 160°C/325°F/gas 3. Take one-third of the dough out of the fridge, remove the cling film and roll it out to a thickness of 5 mm. Cut out circles using a 5-cm cookie cutter. Place on the baking sheet and bake for 25–30 minutes until medium brown in colour; monitor them closely as they can burn very quickly. Remove from the oven and transfer onto wire racks to cool. Repeat with the other two-thirds of the dough.

To make the lemon glaze, sieve the icing sugar into a bowl. Gradually add the lemon juice, 1 teaspoon to start off with, then almost drop by drop, stirring in between each addition to make sure the glaze doesn't get too runny. The glaze should be of a spreadable consistency.

Store the gingerbread in airtight containers and glaze either immediately or up to three days after baking. They will take about four weeks to soften and be at their most flavourful. The biscuits can be stored for up to six weeks, mellowing nicely with age.

NOTE

These gingerbread need to be made a minimum of four weeks in advance. They are rock hard when first baked but become soft and nicely chewy over time.

Glaze the gingerbread to your own imagination: give your artistic talent full reign during the season of advent! Use a teaspoon to decorate the surface of each gingerbread or glaze the entire surface.

Vanillekipferln

VANILLA SHORTBREAD CRESCENTS

MAKES 48

FOR THE SHORTBREAD

280 g plain flour

50 g icing sugar

210 g unsalted butter, cold

100 g ground almonds

2 large egg yolks

FOR THE COATING

250 g icing sugar

5 tbsp homemade vanilla sugar (see below)

40 g caster sugar

Preheat the oven to 190°C/375°F/gas 5. Line a baking sheet with baking parchment.

Start by making the biscuits. Sieve the flour into a food processor and add the icing sugar. Dice the butter, add to the flour and process until the mixture resembles coarse breadcrumbs. Add the ground almonds and the egg yolks and process again. Turn the mixture onto a clean, floured work surface and, using your hands, mix swiftly into a smooth dough.

Wrap the dough in cling film and refrigerate for one hour. After this time, remove from the fridge, discard the cling film and break off small walnut-size pieces of dough. On a clean work surface, roll them into 1 x 6-cm rolls. Bend into half-moons (crescents) and place onto the prepared baking sheet. Bake for 18–20 minutes, until golden.

In the meantime, prepare the coating. Sieve all three sugars into a large bowl and mix well.

When cooked, remove the crescents from the oven and immediately tip them into the coating, carefully rolling them in the sugar to coat them all over. This is an art indeed, as you have to work quickly while the crescents are still hot! You may have to work in batches, depending on the size of your bowl.

Once the crescents are all coated and still a little warm, place them into a biscuit tin with a tight-fitting lid, placing a sheet of waxed paper between each layer. Let them cool in the tin with the lid on. Store for up to four weeks. Not suitable for freezing.

HOMEMADE VANILLA SUGAR

To make your own homemade vanilla sugar, run the blade of a sharp knife down the length of a vanilla pod to split it open. Cut these two lengths again. Do not scrape out the seeds! Place the split pods into a 250-ml glass jar filled with icing sugar. The icing sugar will take on the flavour of the vanilla within about one month and produce a lovely aromatic flavour. Vanilla sugar keeps for up to 6 months in a sealed jar and can be used as a replacement for the packaged variety, which has very little flavour.

Tiroler Klosterkipferln Tatjana

TATJANA'S TIROLIAN CONVENT CRESCENTS

MAKES 24

140 g plain flour

40 g icing sugar

100 g unsalted butter, cold

90 g ground roasted hazelnuts (see box)

1 tsp homemade vanilla sugar (see page 136), or ½ tsp vanilla extract

40 g dark (70% cocoa) chocolate, grated

1 tbsp mixed peel, very finely chopped

1 large egg yolk

100 g plain (50% cocoa) chocolate, melted

Sieve the flour with the icing sugar into a food processor and add the butter, diced. Process until the mixture resembles coarse breadcrumbs. Add the ground hazelnuts, vanilla, grated chocolate and the mixed peel and egg yolk and process briefly again. Turn the mixture out onto a clean floured work surface and, using your hands, mix swiftly into a smooth dough.

Wrap the dough in cling film and refrigerate for one hour. Preheat the oven to 180°C/350°F/gas 4. Line a baking sheet with baking parchment.

After this time, remove from the fridge, discard the cling film and break off small walnut-size pieces of dough. On a clean work surface, roll them into 1 x 6-cm rolls. Bend into half-moons (crescents) and place onto the prepared baking sheet. Bake for 18–20 minutes, until golden. Remove from the oven and set aside to cool.

When cooled, dip both ends of the crescents into the melted chocolate and place on wax paper until the chocolate hardens. Store in airtight containers for up to four weeks. Not suitable for freezing.

ROASTING HAZELNUTS

Spread out the hazelnuts on a baking tray and place in a preheated 150°C/300°F/gas 2 oven. Toast for about 10 minutes until fragrant, watching that they don't burn (check one by removing the skin to see that there is a shade of colour). Remove from the oven, place in a clean kitchen towel and rub the nuts together until the skins come off. Pulse the nuts briefly in a food processor.

Süße Mehlspeisen

SWEET DESSERTS

When I was a child visiting my Austrian grandmother, I was always excited when a *Süße Mehlspeise* was on the menu, a main course that although sweet, is often served as a light meal for lunch or an early dinner. An example would be a meal consisting of *Kaiserschmarren* (see page 148), a type of thick pancake, chopped into small pieces and dusted with powdered sugar. Or a *Marillenknödel* (see page 146), a wonderfully aromatic and delicious sweet dumpling filled with the ripest of apricots (or plums) in season, rolled in buttered breadcrumbs and sprinkled with sugar. They are filled with the purest nostalgia of a warm late July summer's day.

Perhaps the fruit justified the nutritional value of these dishes, but the memories of them, especially given my North American upbringing, always came with a slightly decadent feeling of eating something you really shouldn't be. Anyone who has grown up in Austria like my mother will also vividly recall these summer specialities.

Süße Mehlspeisen also incorporate sweetened breads and cakes, such as the famed *Gugelhupf* (see page 156), a plum tart or jam-filled doughnuts. These, however, remain strictly intended for tea or coffee breaks.

Apfelknödel

APPLE DUMPLINGS

SERVES 4

FOR THE DUMPLINGS

1 kg dessert apples, peeled, cored and finely cubed

1 tbsp granulated sugar

2 tbsp semolina

1 large egg

150–180 g plain flour

FOR THE COATING

120 g unsalted butter

150 g fine breadcrumbs

30 g granulated sugar

Start by making the dumplings. Put the cubed apples in a bowl, stirring in the sugar and semolina and let stand for 1–2 hours, covered.

After this time, mix the egg into the apples. With a wooden spoon, stir in enough of the flour (starting with 150 g, then adding up to 30 g more) to reach the consistency of dough.

Bring a large pan of lightly salted water to the boil. With hands wet, scoop out a level tablespoon of the dough and roll it gently in the palms of your hands to form a ball, slightly smaller than the size of a golf ball. You will need to wet your hands regularly so that the dumplings don't stick to them.

Drop the dumplings into the boiling water, one at a time (you will need to cook them in batches as it is likely they won't all fit in the pan at the same time). The dumplings will sink to the bottom of the pan. Partially cover the pan and when the water has returned to the boil, lower the heat to a simmer. After 10–12 minutes, the dumplings will be ready and will have floated to the top. Simmer for another 2–3 minutes, then lift them out with a slotted spoon and into a colander to drain.

To make the coating, melt the butter in a large frying pan and fry the breadcrumbs until lightly browned. Add the drained dumplings and roll them in the crumb mixture for a couple of minutes so that they are evenly coated. Place this first batch of dumplings in a warmed 150°C/300°F/gas 3 oven while waiting for the second batch to cook.

Transfer the dumplings onto warmed plates, sprinkling liberally with the sugar and serve immediately. A stewed fresh fruit compote complements these dumplings perfectly.

Apfelschmarren Nora

NORA'S APPLE PANCAKE

MAKES 8 SLICES

2 large eggs

375 ml full-fat milk

120 g plain flour

1 tsp granulated sugar, depending on sweetness of fruit

Pinch of salt

60 g unsalted butter

750 g dessert apples (or 500 g apples and 250 g pears), peeled, cored and thinly sliced

Icing sugar, for dusting

Preheat the oven to 200°C/400°F/gas 6.

In the bowl of an electric mixer, beat the eggs until light. Then add the milk, flour, sugar and salt, and beat on a lower speed to a thin batter.

Melt the butter in a 33 x 23 cm cast-iron roasting tin in the oven: it should be hot and bubbling but make sure it's not burning. Remove from the oven and spread the apples evenly in the tin, then return to the oven and bake for 20 minutes, until the apples are half cooked. Give them a good stir, then pour the batter over the top. Increase the oven temperature to 220°C/425°F/gas 7 and bake for another 15 minutes, until well-puffed and golden on top.

Place the tin onto a wire rack and cool for a few minutes. Dust with icing sugar and cut into eight pieces before serving.

Béchamelstrudel

BÉCHAMEL STRUDEL

MAKES 8 SLICES

1 x 250-g packet of ready-made filo pastry

50 g butter, melted, for brushing

FOR THE BÉCHAMEL

3 tbsp butter

3 tbsp plain flour

200 ml whipping cream

4 large eggs, separated

1 tbsp soured milk

80 g caster sugar

50 g sultanas

FOR THE VANILLA SAUCE

2 large egg yolks

500 ml milk

50 g granulated sugar

½ vanilla pod

Start by making the béchamel. Melt the butter in a heavy-base saucepan, then whisk in the flour and cook for about a minute, until bubbling. Remove from the heat, add the whipping cream, while stirring rapidly with a wooden spoon. Return to the heat, bring to the boil, while stirring vigorously, then reduce to a simmer and cook for another 2 minutes.

Transfer the béchamel to a large bowl. When cooled, add the egg yolks, one at a time, beating well after each addition. Stir in the soured cream and sugar.

Preheat the oven to 180°C/350°F/gas 4. Position the rack in the upper third of the oven. Line a swiss roll tin with baking parchment.

In a separate bowl, beat the egg whites to stiff peaks. Unwrap the filo pastry sheets and lay them out onto a clean work surface. Working quickly, brush the first sheet with melted butter and position another sheet immediately on top, overlapping the first sheet slightly. Repeat with another sheet of filo pastry, until you have a rectangle about 26 x 18 cm. Gently fold the egg whites into the béchamel using a spatula and spread down the centre of the pastry sheet. Sprinkle the sultanas over the filling and brush the edges of the pastry sheet with melted butter. Roll up into a strudel shape.

Transfer carefully onto the prepared tray, shape into a crescent and brush the top and sides with the remaining butter. Bake for 45–55 minutes, until crisp and light brown but check the colour after 35 minutes. Best served warm and with a vanilla sauce.

To make the vanilla sauce, whisk all the ingredients together in a medium heat-resistant bowl. Set over a pan of simmering water, being careful that the bowl does not touch the water. Whisk for at least 5 minutes, until thick and pale (the mixture should double in volume). Remove the vanilla pod.

Marillenknödel (oder Zwetchenknödel)

APRICOT (OR PLUM) DUMPLINGS

MAKES 12

FOR THE DUMPLINGS

1 kg floury potatoes

250 g plain flour, plus extra for dusting (or 200 g flour and 50 g semolina)

40 g unsalted butter, diced

1 tsp salt

1 large egg

1 kg very small ripe apricots or 1 kg of small ripe plums

FOR THE COATING

120 g unsalted butter

150 g plain breadcrumbs

FOR DUSTING

30 g caster sugar (if using apricots)

30 g caster sugar mixed with 1 tsp ground cinnamon (if using plums)

Start by making the dumplings. Boil the potatoes in their skins and when cool enough to handle, peel them and cut them in half. Flour a clean work surface and mash the potatoes in a potato ricer directly onto the floured surface.

Sieve the flour and semolina, if using, onto a floured surface. Add the diced butter and use your fingertips to combine, pinching until the mixture resembles coarse crumbs. Add the salt and the cooled, mashed potatoes and lightly mix. Tip the mixture out onto a floured work surface, make a well in the centre of the mixture and add the egg. Knead the dough with your hands to form a soft dough, making sure not to overwork it. Cut the dough into two as it will be easier to handle when rolling.

Shape the dough into a roll about 5 cm in diameter. Cut it into 12 equal rounds, flatten each piece between your hands and place one apricot in each centre. Wrap the dough around the fruit to completely encase it. Make sure there are no exposed parts of the fruit. Gently roll it into a smooth ball in the palm of your hand.

Bring a large pan of very lightly salted water to the boil. Drop the dumplings into the boiling water, one at a time (you will need to cook them in batches as it is likely they won't all fit in the pan at the same time). The dumplings will sink to the bottom of the pan. Partially cover the pan and when the water has returned to the boil, lower the heat to a simmer. After 10–15 minutes, the dumplings will be ready and will have floated to the top. Lift them out with a slotted spoon and into a colander to drain.

To make the coating, melt the butter in a frying pan and fry the breadcrumbs until lightly browned. Add the dumplings and roll them in the crumb mixture for a couple of minutes so that they are evenly coated. Place this first batch of dumplings in a warmed oven while waiting for the second batch to cook.

Transfer the dumplings onto warmed plates, sprinkling liberally with the sugar and serve immediately.

Kaiserschmarren

EMPEROR'S MESS

SERVES 2

125 g plain flour

Pinch of salt

250 ml milk

4 large eggs, separated

50 g butter

30 g icing sugar

Icing sugar, for dusting

In a large bowl, mix the flour and salt, add the milk and whisk until smooth. Add 1 egg yolk at a time, whisking well between additions.

In a separate bowl, beat the egg whites until very stiff. Fold them gently into the batter using a balloon whisk until well incorporated.

Heat a cast-iron frying pan over a medium to high heat. Melt a heaped tablespoon of the butter until it bubbles. Quickly add about one-third of the batter to cover the bottom of the pan, distributing it evenly and immediately reducing the heat to low. Cover with a lid for 2½ minutes, then check to see if the bottom is golden. If it is, turn the pancake over and add a little more of the butter into the pan. It doesn't matter if the pancake breaks up while you're flipping it. Cover with the lid once more and after 1–2 minutes, check if the underside is golden. Sieve one-third of the icing sugar over the pancake.

Using two tablespoons, roughly tear the dough into 2–4-cm pieces, and stir the pieces for a few minutes in the pan so that they become golden on all sides. Transfer to a serving plate to keep warm. Repeat twice more with the remaining two-thirds of the batter, or until all of the batter has been used. Serve while hot and crisp on warmed plates and dust with icing sugar. Kaiserschmarren is traditionally served with stewed plums, or any other stewed fruit.

Kaiserschmarren is a beloved Austrian dish served as a dessert or main meal. *Kaiser*, meaning Emperor in German, and *Schmarrn*, Austrian slang for a kind of mishmash or poppycock, provides us with the charming literal translation of 'the Emperor's mess', referring to Emperor Franz Josef I, who ruled Austria from 1848 to 1916. Speculation as to the origins of the dish are varied, but a popular favourite is that it was inadvertently created by the Emperor's cook. Whenever the Emperor's pancakes did not turn out perfectly because they were too thick or because they tore in the cooking process, they were served to his servants as *Kaiserschmarren*.

Palatschinken
SWEET CRÊPES

MAKES 12

FOR THE CRÊPES

150 g plain flour

250 ml full-fat milk
(or 125 ml milk and
125 ml single cream)

2 large eggs

2 large egg yolks

¼ tsp salt

1 tsp caster sugar

50 g unsalted butter

CURD CHEESE FILLING

50 g unsalted butter

50 g icing sugar

2 large eggs

250 g curd cheese, sieved
through a fine mesh

125 ml soured cream

Grated zest of 1 lemon

50 g sultanas

A little milk

Vanilla sugar (see page 136),
to taste

Jam of your choice (we
favour apricot or raspberry)

Start by making the crêpes. In a large bowl, mix all the ingredients to a batter. Melt a knob of butter in a frying pan over a medium high heat. Pour a small ladleful of batter into the pan. Tilt the pan quickly so that the batter thinly covers the surface of the pan. Fry over a medium heat until golden on one side. Turn over and fry the other side.

Stack the crêpes one on top of each other on a plate and keep warm in a low oven until all crêpes have been cooked.

Spread a thin layer of jam onto each crêpe. Roll them up and serve dusted with vanilla sugar. Alternatively, you can fill them with a curd cheese filling. To make the filling start by preheating the oven to 180°C/350°F/gas 4.

Cream the butter until light using an electric mixer. Add the icing sugar and cream until light and fluffy. Add one egg at a time, beating well between each addition. With a wooden spoon, mix in the sieved curd cheese, soured cream, lemon zest, sultanas, and finally, as much milk as is needed to make a spreadable mixture that is the consistency of jam.

Spread each crêpe with the filling. Fold in quarters and place them in a buttered ovenproof dish and bake for 10–15 minutes.

Buchteln

SWEET JAM BUNS

MAKES 16

20 g compressed yeast

50 g caster sugar

175 ml milk

350 g strong flour

Pinch of salt

2 large egg yolks

60 g unsalted butter, melted and cooled

Grated zest of ½ lemon and ½ orange

80–100 g jam, such as apricot or plum (see page 219)

40 g unsalted butter, melted

Icing sugar, for dusting

Make sure all the ingredients and kitchen equipment are at room temperature.

Cream the yeast with 1 teaspoon of the sugar and gradually add the milk. Set in a warm place to prove: a preheated 100°C/212°F/¼ gas oven that has been turned off works well for this purpose.

Sift the flour with the salt into a warmed bowl.

In a separate bowl, whisk the egg yolks and the remaining sugar, and stir this into the flour with the yeast mixture, just as it starts to bubble and has risen to double its size. Mix in the butter and lemon and orange zest and beat with a wooden spoon, until the dough begins to 'blister' (i.e. it has a satiny sheen and pulls away from the bowl). Turn the dough out onto a floured work surface and knead it until it feels smooth and elastic, for about 7–10 minutes. Add a little flour if the dough sticks to the surface. Shape into a ball and transfer it into an oiled bowl, rolling the ball around to coat it lightly in the oil. Cover with a clean tea towel.

Set the dough in a warm place, away from any drafts, ideally near a sun-lit spot. Leave to rise for 1–1¼ hours, until doubled in size: the length of time this takes depends on the room temperature and the temperature of the ingredients and tools, being used.

When the dough has doubled in size, transfer it to a floured work surface. Knead it for a few seconds and roll it into a 1-cm thick rectangle. Cut into 16 6-cm squares. Put 1 teaspoon of jam in the centre of each square. Gather the four corners and pinch them together to encase its contents.

Dip each packet into the melted butter, keeping some of the butter in reserve, and then place, sealed-sides down, onto a warmed, well-buttered 27-cm round cast-iron dish. The buns should crowd and touch each other in the pan. Cover with a tea towel and leave to rise in a warm place once more for about 45–60 minutes. Preheat the oven to 190°C/375°F/gas 5.

Just prior to baking, brush the tops of the buns with the remaining melted butter and bake in the oven for 25–30 minutes until the buns pull away from the sides of the baking dish, and are golden brown on top. Immediately turn them over onto a wire rack to cool then dust with icing sugar and separate them to serve.

Gebackene Mäuse

DEEP-FRIED 'MICE'

MAKES 21

20 g compressed yeast

40 g granulated sugar

200 ml tepid full-fat milk

350 g plain flour

½ tsp salt

1 large egg

50 g unsalted butter, melted and cooled

Grated zest of 1 lemon

50 g sultanas, soaked in 1–2 tbsp light rum for 30 minutes

Sunflower (or canola) oil, for deep-frying

Icing sugar, for dusting

Make sure all the ingredients and kitchen equipment are at room temperature.

Cream the yeast with 1 teaspoon of the sugar and gradually add the milk. Set in a warm place to prove: a preheated 100°C/212°F/¼ gas oven that has been turned off works well for this purpose.

Sift the flour with the salt into a warmed bowl.

In a separate bowl, whisk the egg and the remaining sugar, and stir this into the flour with the yeast mixture, just as it starts to bubble and has risen to double its size. Mix in the butter and lemon zest and beat with a wooden spoon, until the dough has a satiny sheen and pulls away from the bowl. Turn the dough out onto a floured work surface and knead it until it feels smooth and elastic, for about 7–10 minutes. Add a little flour if the dough sticks to the surface. Mix in the drained sultanas. Shape into a ball and transfer it into an oiled bowl, rolling the ball around to coat it lightly in the oil. Cover with a clean tea towel. A more welcoming, less labour-intensive option should it be available, is to use an electric mixer with a dough hook.

Set the dough in a warm place, away from any drafts, ideally near a sun-lit spot. Leave to rise for 1–1½ hours, until doubled in size: the length of time this takes depends on the room temperature and the temperature of the ingredients and tools, being used.

Heat the oil in a deep-fryer to a temperature of 157°C–163°C (315°F–325°F). When the dough has doubled in size, punch it down once with your fist to deflate. Dip a tablespoon into the hot oil and scoop out a portion of dough. Slide the dough from the oily spoon onto a dry tablespoon and then let the dough glide into the hot oil. It will slide off the spoon easily. Continue in this manner with as many spoonfuls as will fit the pan without overcrowding. When the dough hits the oil and loses some of its shape little creatures resembling mice with small curly tails will form.

Turn the 'mice' over with tongs once the underside has turned a deep golden colour and wait for the other side to colour. Don't rush this step! Test one by breaking it in half to see if the inside is fully baked with no trace of raw dough. Lift out the golden mice with a slotted spoon or tongs, drain on paper towels set over a wire rack. Dust with icing sugar when the mice have cooled slightly. They are best served warm.

Mohnbeugel

POPPY-SEED CRESCENTS

MAKES 18

FOR THE FILLING

125 ml full-fat milk

80 g caster sugar

120 g ground poppy
seed

Grated zest of 1 small lemon

20 g sultanas soaked in
2 tsp rum for 30 minutes

Pinch of ground cinnamon

FOR THE DOUGH

15 g compressed yeast

60 ml full-fat milk, cold

250 g strong flour

Pinch of salt

120 g unsalted butter,
at room temperature

20 g caster sugar

1 large egg yolk

1 large egg, for brushing

Start by making the filling. In a saucepan, bring the milk and sugar to a gentle boil. Stir in the poppy seeds, then reduce the heat to a simmer and stir regularly for 15 minutes. Remove from the heat and stir in the lemon zest, rum-soaked sultanas and the cinnamon. Set aside to cool.

To prepare the dough, dissolve the yeast in the milk. Sieve the flour onto a clean work surface and add the salt. Cut in the butter with a knife and crumble with your fingertips until the mixture resembles coarse crumbs. Mix in the sugar and make a well in the centre. Add the egg yolk with the dissolved yeast mixture and stir with the knife and then begin to gather all the ingredients into a ball with your hands, kneading it into a smooth dough. Leave the dough to rest on the work surface for 45 minutes covered with a clean tea towel.

After the resting period, knead the dough briefly and form it into a 25-cm long log. Cut it in half lengthways and divide each half into nine equal rounds with a sharp knife. Place each round onto a lightly floured work surface. Using only the ball of your hand, spread the shape into an oval the size of a good-sized palm. Place a small teaspoon of the filling in the centre of the dough, then fold over the dough and press the edges together. Shape into crescents and place each piece 7-cm apart onto a baking sheet lined with baking parchment, making sure the seams are face down. Brush the surface of each crescent with beaten egg, then leave them to rise in a warm place for 45 minutes.

Preheat the oven to 180°C/350°F/gas 4. Bake the crescents for 18–20 minutes until golden brown. Remove from the oven and transfer onto wire racks to cool.

Gugelhupf mit Germ

YEAST-BASED GUGELHUPF

SERVES 6

50 g flaked almonds

20 g compressed yeast

80 g caster sugar

250 ml tepid milk

500 g plain flour, sifted

250 g unsalted butter,
at room temperature

3 large egg yolks

1 large egg

Grated zest of 1–2 lemons,
to taste

Pinch of salt

80 g sultanas, floured

Vanilla sugar (see page 136)
or icing sugar, for dusting

Make sure all the ingredients and kitchen equipment are at room temperature. The yeast can be set on top of the cooker to warm.

Grease and lightly flour a ring mould. Sprinkle with the flaked almonds, which should stick to the sides.

Cream the yeast with a teaspoon of the sugar and about three-quarters of the tepid milk and one teaspoon of the flour. Mix and set it aside in a warm place to rise for 15–20 minutes.

In the bowl of an electric mixer, cream the butter, gradually adding in the sugar. Add one egg yolk at time, beating well between each addition. Then beat in the whole egg. Stir in the grated lemon zest, salt and a little of the flour, then the yeast mixture and the remaining flour and milk. Beat well with a wooden spoon until the dough comes off the sides of the bowl. If done by hand, this should take about 5 minutes. Add the sultanas. Distribute the dough into the mould. Cover with a dry, clean tea towel and place in warm place to rise until the dough comes to within 2.5 cm of the top of the mould. This should take 50–60 minutes.

Preheat the oven to 180°C/350°F/gas 4. Bake for 50–60 minutes, but reduce the heat to 120°C/250°F/gas ½ for the last 20 minutes.

Remove from oven and turn over onto a wire rack. Dust liberally with vanilla sugar or icing sugar and cover with a tea towel to cool completely.

Traditionally, there's an option to make a Gugelhupf either with yeast or with baking powder. Though yeast sounds a little more complicated, the flavour is much more satisfying. In Hertha's bygone era cooks would sit with bowls between their laps and work the dough for what seemed like hours. Today, a packet of yeast and a food processor make life much easier, and the taste identical.

Kärtner Reindling

CARINTHIAN RING CAKE

SERVES 6

FOR THE DOUGH

20 g compressed yeast

60 g granulated sugar

175 ml milk

350 g strong flour

Pinch of salt

1 large egg yolk

70 g unsalted butter, melted and cooled

Grated zest of 1 lemon

FOR THE FILLING

50 g figs or prunes, chopped

50 g walnuts, chopped

50 g sultanas

30 g candied orange peel or mixed peel

20 g dark brown soft sugar

1 tsp ground cinnamon

20 g unsalted butter, melted

FOR THE GLAZE (OPTIONAL)

125 icing sugar

3–4 tbsp rum

Make sure all the ingredients and kitchen equipment are at room temperature.

Generously grease and flour a deep, 25-cm round cast-iron casserole.

Start by making the dough. Cream the yeast with one teaspoon of the sugar and the milk. Leave in a warm place to prove for 8–10 minutes. The yeast can be set on top of the cooker to warm.

Sift the flour with the salt into a warmed bowl. In a separate bowl, whisk the egg yolk and the remaining sugar, and stir this into the flour with the yeast mixture, just as it begins to bubble and has risen to double its size. Mix in the butter and lemon zest and beat with a wooden spoon, until the dough begins to 'blister' (i.e. it has a satiny sheen and pulls away from the bowl). Turn the dough out onto a floured work surface and knead it until it feels smooth and elastic, for about 7–10 minutes. Add a little flour if the dough sticks to the surface. Shape into a ball and transfer it into an oiled bowl, rolling the ball around to coat it lightly in the oil. Cover with a clean tea towel. A more welcoming, less labour-intensive option should it be available, is to use an electric mixer with a dough hook.

Set the dough in a warm place, away from any drafts, ideally near a sun-lit spot. Leave to rise for 45–60 minutes, or until doubled in size: the length of time this takes depends on the room temperature of the ingredients and tools being used.

In the meantime, mix all the ingredients for the filling together, minus the melted butter, and set aside.

Once the dough has doubled in size, roll it out on to a floured work surface to a 5-mm thick rectangle 23 x 40 cm in size. Sprinkle the filling over the dough, leaving a 2 cm border all round, then dribble the melted butter over the filling. Using a rolling pin, gently press the filling into the dough. Roll up the dough lengthways into a cylinder, pressing the seam to seal it.

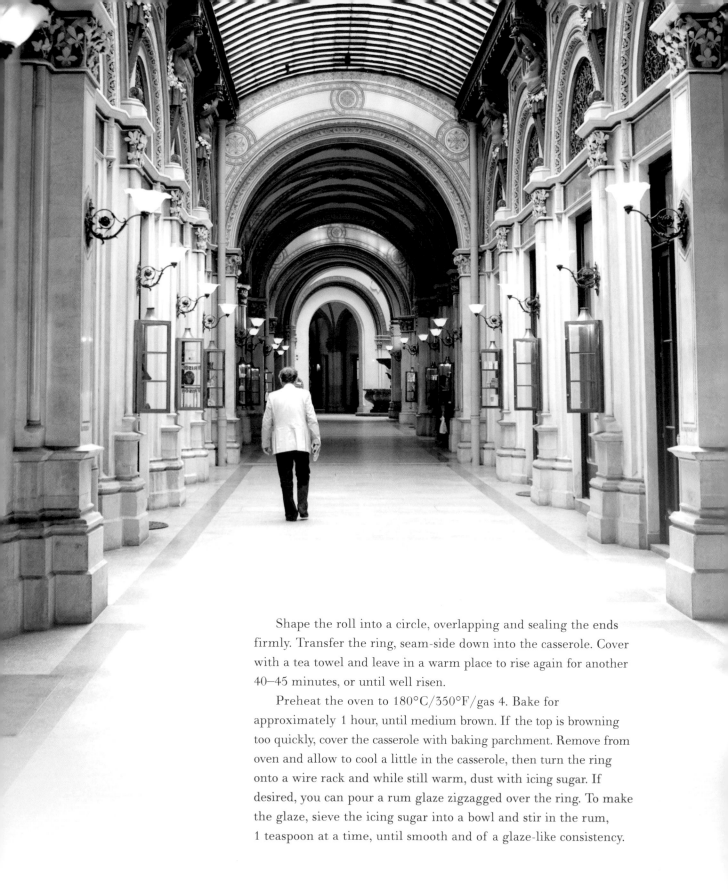

Shape the roll into a circle, overlapping and sealing the ends firmly. Transfer the ring, seam-side down into the casserole. Cover with a tea towel and leave in a warm place to rise again for another 40–45 minutes, or until well risen.

Preheat the oven to 180°C/350°F/gas 4. Bake for approximately 1 hour, until medium brown. If the top is browning too quickly, cover the casserole with baking parchment. Remove from oven and allow to cool a little in the casserole, then turn the ring onto a wire rack and while still warm, dust with icing sugar. If desired, you can pour a rum glaze zigzagged over the ring. To make the glaze, sieve the icing sugar into a bowl and stir in the rum, 1 teaspoon at a time, until smooth and of a glaze-like consistency.

Zwetschkengermfleck

PLUM CAKE

SERVES 6

20 g compressed yeast

70 g granulated sugar

175 ml full-fat tepid milk

350 g strong flour

Pinch of salt

1 large egg yolk

Grated zest of 1 lemon

60 g unsalted butter, softened

300 g small plums, washed, quartered and stones removed

Egg white, for brushing

Icing sugar, for dusting (optional)

In a warm bowl, mix the yeast with one teaspoon of the sugar. Add a little of the tepid milk to form a paste. Add the rest of the milk with one teaspoon of the flour. Set aside to rise in a warm place for about 8–10 minutes.

In a large warmed bowl, sift the remaining flour, salt, the remaining sugar, egg yolk, lemon zest and the risen yeast. Lastly, add the softened butter. Using a wooden spoon, beat until the dough becomes shiny and pulls away from the wooden spoon and the sides of the bowl. Cover the bowl with a clean tea towel and leave it to rise in a warm place until almost doubled in size. This should take about 50 minutes.

Grease and lightly flour a 37 x 25 cm baking tray that is about 2.5 cm deep. When the dough has risen, knead it briefly on a floured surface. Take two-thirds of the dough, and with the palms of your wet hands, stretch it carefully out over the surface of the tin. The dough should be quite thin. Place the plums on the dough in rows so that they are touching each other and cover the surface of the dough.

Prepare a lattice with the remaining third of the dough. This is optional as it is time-consuming, but very traditional and makes the cake look very pretty. Roll out the dough and make thin rolls about the thickness of a finger and place over the plums in a lattice pattern. Brush the tops of lattice with egg white. Let it rise once more for 30 minutes. Preheat the oven to 190°C/375°F/gas 5.

Bake for about 35–40 minutes, until the top is golden brown and the plums are thoroughly cooked. For an extra-sweet touch, dust with icing sugar while the cake is still warm.

Streuselkuchen

CRUMBLE CAKE

SERVES 6

FOR THE DOUGH

10 g fresh compressed yeast

10 g granulated sugar

60 ml full-fat tepid milk

140 g strong flour

Pinch of salt

2 egg yolks

30 g unsalted butter, melted and cooled

Grated zest of 1 medium lemon

FOR THE TOPPING

100 g plain flour

40 g ground almonds

50 g dark brown soft sugar

1 tsp ground cinnamon

Grated zest of 1 small lemon

60 g unsalted butter, melted

Grease and flour a 7-cm deep, 25-cm square cast-iron baking dish.

Start by making the dough. Cream the yeast with one teaspoon of the sugar and milk. Set aside to prove for 8–10 minutes.

Sift the flour with the salt into a warm bowl. Make a well in the centre and add the egg yolks, remaining sugar, cooled melted butter, lemon zest and the proven yeast. Mix and beat with a wooden spoon for about 10–15 minutes, until the dough becomes smooth and shiny. Using the dough hook on an electric mixer will simplify this arduous procedure.

Shape the dough into a ball and cover the bowl with a clean tea towel. Leave it in a warm place to rise to double its size. Depending on the room temperature, this will take about 1 hour.

In the meantime, make the topping. Mix all the ingredients together (except for the butter). Then pour the melted butter into the dry mixture and stir gently: the topping should be in the form of clumps.

Once the dough has risen, punch it down with your fist to deflate and knead it briefly on a floured surface. Place it into the prepared baking dish, using your knuckles to press it into all four corners. Sprinkle the topping evenly to cover the dough. Cover with a clean tea towel and set it aside to rise once more for 45–60 minutes, until doubled in size.

Preheat the oven to 190°C/375°F/gas 5. Bake for 35–45 minutes, then remove from the oven and carefully remove the cake from the dish.

Kuchen und Schnitten

CAKES AND GÂTEAUX

For me, cakes and gâteaux seemed initially daunting to attempt, but for my Austrian mother, they come as naturally as breathing and are made with the precision and delicacy of a surgeon. High-quality ingredients such as fresh hazelnuts and almonds, cinnamon, sultanas, cloves and seasonal fruits like cherries, apples and plums provide pure, refined and rich yet delicate tastes. Once you learn that egg whites are only whipped on their own or with a little bit of sugar and only ever gently folded into a batter, that butter is creamed, with the magic words *until light and fluffy*, that chocolate must always be dark and of the highest quality, and that a springform tin is as essential as fresh farm eggs and unsalted butter, then you are, well, almost half-way there.

Apfelschlangel Elsa

ELSA'S APPLE SLICES

SERVES 6–8

FOR THE DOUGH

180 g plain flour

1 tsp baking powder

80 g unsalted butter, cold, plus extra for greasing

60 g caster sugar

1 large egg

FOR THE FILLING

750 g Bramley apples, peeled, cored and finely sliced

100 g granulated sugar

50 g sultanas

Grated zest of one lemon

1 egg white

Icing sugar, for dusting

Preheat the oven to 180°C/350°F/gas 4. Line a 25 x 38 cm baking tray with baking parchment.

Start by making the dough. All ingredients for the dough should be cold. Sieve the flour along with the baking powder into a food processor and then add the butter, diced. Process until the mixture resembles coarse breadcrumbs. Mix in the sugar, then add the egg to form a dough which can be easily rolled out. Shape the dough into a ball, wrap it in cling film and refrigerate for at least 30 minutes.

To make the filling, heat a frying pan on a medium to low heat and 'fry' the apples (without any oil or butter) until most of the moisture has evaporated. Set aside to cool. Just before spreading the filling, stir in the sugar, sultanas and lemon zest.

Remove the dough from the fridge and roll it out so that it is slightly longer than the baking sheet and about 5 mm thick. Carefully transfer the dough onto the lined baking sheet so that it is slightly overhanging the sheet.

Spread the cold apple filling along the centre, lengthways. Fold over the short ends by 3 cm on each side, then lift one long end up and over the filling, brush it with egg white and fold the other long end over so it overlaps the centre. Press down gently along the seam. Make sure all is well sealed and tucked in so that none of the mixture can escape. Bake for 40–45 minutes until golden.

Dust generously with icing sugar once cooled. Cut into slices and serve with a dollop of whipped cream (optional).

Apfelstrudel

APPLE STRUDEL

MAKES 12 SLICES

FOR THE PASTRY

250 g plain flour, plus extra for dusting

1 heaped tsp butter, at room temperature

125 ml warm water

Pinch of salt

1 tsp white wine vinegar

1 large egg

50 g butter, melted, for brushing

FOR THE FILLING

100 g plain breadcrumbs, pan-fried in a little butter and cooled

1 kg Bramley apples, peeled, cored and very thinly sliced

100 g granulated sugar

Pinch of ground cinnamon

50 g sultanas

100 g unsalted butter, melted

icing sugar, for dusting

Sift the flour on to a work surface and make a well in the centre. Place the butter into the warm water and pour it into the well along with the salt, vinegar and the egg. Work it in using the tip of a knife, then use your hands to incorporate all the flour. If the mixture is too dry, add a little more warm water. Form into a ball.

Flour the work surface and knead the pastry for 5–7 minutes, by picking it up and throwing it down until it is shiny and smooth. Gather into a ball and cover with a large upturned bowl. Leave to rest for at least 30 minutest to 1 hour. Preheat the oven to 180°C/350°F/ gas 4. Line a baking sheet with baking parchment.

Cover a table with a cotton sheet and lightly sprinkle it with flour. Place the pastry in the centre and roll it out as far as it will go into a circle. Sparingly brush the melted butter around the edges of the rolled out pastry. Carefully slide your hands between the pastry and the sheet. Starting at the centre and working outwards, stretch the pastry out with the backs of your hands. Don't worry about any small tears. Continue to work outwards into all directions, as the pastry becomes almost paper-thin.

Cover two-thirds of the pastry (leaving one-third at the top uncovered), first with the breadcrumbs, then with the apples, sugar, cinnamon and sultanas. Brush the uncovered one-third with the melted butter, reserving some for glazing the top. Cut away any rough edges. Roll it up with the help of the sheet, starting at the filled end, as you would with a Swiss roll.

Carefully transfer the roll to the baking sheet, shaping it like a horseshoe. Brush the top with the remaining melted butter and bake for 40–45 minutes until golden and crisp. Serve warm, sprinkled generously with icing sugar.

> NOTE
> Ready-made filo pastry makes a good, if not entirely authentic, alternative to making your own strudel dough.

Baiserschnitten

MERINGUE BARS

MAKES 8

FOR THE DOUGH

175 g plain flour

½ tsp baking powder

Pinch of salt

2 tbsp icing sugar

1 tsp ground cinnamon

100 g unsalted butter, cold

Grated zest of ½ lemon

2 large egg yolks

Scant 2 tbsp ice-cold water

FOR THE MERINGUE

50 g sultanas

50 g currants

50 g blanched almonds

Grated zest of ½ lemon

2 large egg whites

100 g caster sugar

200 g redcurrant jam for
brushing over pastry

Chill the flour in a bowl for 30 minutes before making the dough. Then sieve the cold flour into a food processor with the baking powder, salt, icing sugar and cinnamon. Dice the butter, add to the flour and process until the mixture resembles coarse breadcrumbs.

Add the lemon zest and process again. Tip the mixture out onto a clean work surface and create a small well in the centre. Using the blade of a knife, mix in the egg yolks with 1 tablespoon of the ice-cold water to bring the dough together. Using your hands, knead swiftly, until incorporated. At this stage, it may be necessary to add part or all of the remaining water (the dough should be pliable but not too soft). Shape into a ball and flatten slightly. Place on a plate, cover with cling film and refrigerate for 30 minutes.

Preheat the oven to 190°C/375°F/gas 5. Line a 37 x 25 cm baking sheet with baking parchment.

In a small saucepan warm the redcurrant jam, then set aside to cool.

Take the dough out of the fridge, remove the cling film and roll it out to the size of the baking sheet, minus 2.5 cm on each long side. Cut the dough lengthways into three equal strips and transfer each strip onto the baking sheet, leaving a gap between each strip. Lightly prick the surface of the dough with a fork and bake for 20–25 minutes, until golden and only partially baked.

Meanwhile, make the meringue. Chop the sultanas, currants, almonds and lemon zest to a medium-fine consistency. Alternatively, you can whiz them very quickly in a food processor but be mindful not to over-process them into a paste.

In a medium bowl, whisk the egg whites to soft peaks using an electric mixer, then add the sugar, one tablespoon at a time, whisking all the while until two-thirds of the sugar has been incorporated and the whites start to look glossy. Fold in the remaining sugar using a large metal spoon. Fold the chopped fruits and almonds into the meringue using a spatula or metal spoon.

Remove the partially baked pastry from the oven and turn the temperature down to 140°C/275°F/gas 1.

Brush a thin layer of the cooled redcurrant jelly over each pastry strip. Equally distribute the meringue mixture over the strips, using a spatula to even out the mixture. Return to the oven and bake for another 30 minutes, until the meringue is tinged with colour and feels firm to the touch.

Remove from the oven, allow to cool, then cut into 5-cm slices using a sharp knife. Store in airtight containers for up to 3 days.

Blitzkuchen

LIGHTNING CAKE

MAKES 12 SLICES

FOR THE BASE
6 large egg yolks
160 g icing sugar
Juice of 1 lemon
90 g plain flour, sieved
4 large egg whites

FOR THE TOPPING
200 g apricot jam
2 large egg whites
200 g icing sugar
70 g flaked almonds

Preheat the oven to 190°C/375°F/gas 5. Line a 35 x 25 cm baking sheet with baking parchment.

Start by making the base. In the bowl of an electric mixer, whisk the egg yolks with the icing sugar and lemon juice until light and fluffy. Gently stir in the flour. Thoroughly wash the beaters and in a separate bowl, whisk the egg whites until almost stiff and then fold into the batter, using a large balloon whisk until just incorporated. Spread the mixture evenly onto the prepared baking sheet and bake for about 10–15 minutes until light in colour. Remove from oven and set aside to cool.

To make the topping, warm the jam in a saucepan on a low heat, then cool. Spread the cooled jam over the dough. In a bowl, whisk the egg whites to soft peaks, then add the icing sugar, one tablespoon at the time, and whisking all the while until incorporated. Now spread the meringue over the jam, covering it entirely. Sprinkle the flaked almonds over the top and return to the oven for approximately 20 minutes, or until the meringue has set and almonds are very lightly coloured.

This recipe is symbolic as it is the first recipe entry in Tante Hertha's collection. *Blitz* means lightning, but it also connotes fast movement. The preparation may not be quite as 'lightning fast' as some of today's modern recipes, but these sweet delights are well worth the effort.

Braune Apfelschnitten

BROWNED APPLE SLICES

MAKES 8–10 SLICES

FOR THE FILLING

750 g Bramley apples, peeled, cored and coarsely shredded

50 g caster sugar

FOR THE DOUGH

240 g plain flour

160 g unsalted butter, cold

4 tbsp caster sugar

30 g ground almonds

60 g dark (70% cocoa) chocolate, finely grated

2 large egg yolks

1 egg white, for sealing

Homemade vanilla sugar (see page 136), for dusting

Start by making the filling. Dry-fry the apples: heat a frying pan on a medium to low heat and 'fry' the apples (without any oil or butter) until most of the moisture has evaporated. Set aside to cool.

Preheat the oven to 200°C/400°F/gas 6. Line a 25 x 38 cm baking sheet with baking parchment.

To make the dough, sieve the flour onto a clean work surface, then thinly slice the cold butter into the flour. Pinch the mixture between your fingertips until it resembles coarse crumbs. Add the sugar, almonds, chocolate and egg yolks. Work the dough with your fingers, then form into a ball. Roll out to the size of the baking sheet and carefully transfer onto the tin.

Spread the filling along the bottom half of the dough, leaving 3 cm at the sides. Fold over the short ends by 3 cm. Lift one long end up and over the filling, brush with egg white and then fold over the other long end so that it overlaps in the centre. Press down gently along the seams, making sure it is all sealed so none of the mixture can escape.

Bake in the oven for 1 hour, then transfer onto a wire rack to cool. Dust with vanilla sugar and serve warm.

Brauner Kirschkuchen

CHOCOLATE CHERRY CAKE

SERVES 8

50 g sponge fingers

120 g blanched ground almonds

60 g dark chocolate

120 g unsalted butter, at room temperature

100 g icing sugar

4 large egg yolks, at room temperature

2 large eggs, at room temperature

4 large egg whites, at room temperature

300 g whole black Morello cherries, washed and dried (fresh or tinned)

Place the sponge fingers in a food processor and whiz into fine crumbs. Alternatively, you can place them in a plastic food bag and smash them with a rolling pin. Transfer into a bowl and mix in the ground almonds.

Preheat the oven to 180°C/350°F/gas 4. Grease a 22-cm round cake tin and line the bottom with baking parchment.

Break the chocolate into small pieces and place in a heatproof bowl. Melt the chocolate, either by heating in a microwave for 20–30 seconds or by placing the bowl over a pan of just simmering water. Make sure the bowl is not touching the water and monitor carefully. Alternatively you can melt the chocolate the way Hertha would have done (see Note on page 122). Stir the chocolate until smooth and set aside to cool.

In the bowl of an electric mixer, cream the butter until light and fluffy. Gradually whisk in the icing sugar a little at a time. Add the egg yolks, one at the time, whisking between each addition, then add the whole eggs, again one at a time and whisking between each addition. Stir in the cooled melted chocolate and transfer the batter into a very large bowl. Thoroughly wash the beaters. In a separate bowl, whisk the egg whites to fairly stiff peaks.

Using a large balloon whisk, fold one-third of the egg whites into the batter, then fold one-third of the biscuit/almond mixture. Repeat twice more, folding in one-third of the ingredients each time.

Pour the mixture into the prepared cake tin and distribute the cherries evenly on top. Bake for 60–70 minutes, until the cake pulls away from the sides of the tin. Remove from the oven and cool in the tin before transferring to a wire rack. Serve with a generous dollop of whipped cream (see page 179).

Feine Schokoladenschnitten

DELICATE CHOCOLATE SLICES

MAKES 18

20 g sponge fingers

50 g potato or rice flour

150 g dark chocolate

150 g unsalted butter, at room temperature

150 g icing sugar

5 large eggs, separated

250 ml whipping cream, whipped fairly stiffly and lightly sweetened

Preheat the oven to 160°C/320°F/gas 3. Line a 5-cm deep 34 x 22 cm tin with baking parchment and lightly grease the paper.

Place the sponge fingers in a food processor and whiz into fine crumbs. Alternatively, you can place them in a plastic food bag and smash them with a rolling pin. Transfer into a bowl and mix in the flour.

Break the chocolate into small pieces and place in a heatproof bowl. Melt the chocolate, either by heating in a microwave for 20–30 seconds or by placing the bowl over a pan of just simmering water. Make sure the bowl is not touching the water and monitor carefully. Alternatively you can melt the chocolate the way Hertha would have done (see Note on page 122). Stir the chocolate until smooth and set aside to cool.

In the bowl of an electric mixer, cream the butter until light and fluffy. Add the icing sugar, whisking all the time, then the egg yolks, one at a time, whisking between each addition. Stir in the cooled melted chocolate and transfer the batter into a very large bowl. Thoroughly wash the beaters. In a separate bowl, whisk the egg whites to stiff peaks.

Using a large balloon whisk, fold one-third of the egg whites into the batter, then fold one-third of the biscuit/flour mixture. Repeat twice more, folding in one-third of the ingredients each time.

Pour the mixture into the prepared tin. Bake for 20–25 minutes, until the cake pulls away from the sides of the tin. Remove from the oven and turn the cake out onto a wire rack to cool. Cut in half, horizontally, and spread the sweetened whipped cream over the bottom half and cover with the top half.

Mohnkuchen

POPPY SEED TART

SERVES 6

FOR THE DOUGH

150 g plain flour

80 g unsalted butter, cold, and extra for greasing

50 g caster sugar

Pinch ground cinnamon

Grated zest of ½ lemon

1 large egg yolk, beaten

FOR THE FILLING

3 large eggs, separated

120 g icing sugar

120 g ground poppy seeds

20 g sultanas

30 g candied lemon peel, very finely chopped

Grated zest of 1 medium lemon

Icing sugar, for dusting

Lightly grease a 20-cm springform tin.

Sieve the flour on to a clean work surface then thinly slice the cold butter into the flour. Pinch the mixture between your fingertips until it resembles coarse crumbs. Add the sugar, cinnamon, the lemon zest and beaten egg yolk, and swiftly knead everything into a dough, shape into a disc, wrap in cling film and place into the refrigerator to chill for at least 30 minutes and up to 1 hour.

Preheat the oven to 190°C/375°F/gas 5. Remove the pastry from the fridge and let it stand for 5 minutes. Using your knuckles, press the dough into the tin so that it is evenly distributed over the base. If the dough is still too hard, wait just a few more minutes. Bake in the centre of the oven for 10 minutes.

Meanwhile prepare the filling. Whisk the egg yolks with 100 g of the icing sugar until very light and fluffy and transfer to a large bowl. Add the poppy seeds, sultanas, candied lemon peel and the zest. Thoroughly wash the beaters.

In a separate bowl, whip the egg whites to soft peaks, add the remaining icing sugar and whisk to firm, but not stiff, peaks. Gently fold the egg whites into the poppy seed mixture using a spatula.

Remove the partially baked base from the oven and reduce the temperature to 180°C/350°F/gas 4. Pour the filling over the base and return to the oven. Bake for about 45 minutes, until the top turns golden and the cake pulls away from the sides of the tin. Transfer to a cooling rack. Leave in the tin for 5 minutes, before removing the springform ring. Cool completely and dust with icing sugar.

Sacherschnitten

SACHER SLICES

MAKES 10 SLICES

FOR THE BATTER

70–90 g dark chocolate

90 g unsalted butter,
at room temperature

90 g icing sugar

3 large eggs, separated

100 g apricot jam, warmed

40 g plain flour

FOR THE GLAZE

100 g (50% cocoa) chocolate

50 g unsalted butter,
at room temperature

Start by making the batter. Break the chocolate into small pieces and place in a heatproof bowl. Melt the chocolate, either by heating in a microwave for 20–30 seconds or by placing the bowl over a pan of just simmering water. Make sure the bowl is not touching the water and monitor carefully. Alternatively you can melt the chocolate the way Hertha would have done (see Note on page 122). Stir the chocolate until smooth and set aside to cool. Preheat the oven to 180°C/350°F/gas 4.

In the bowl of an electric mixer, cream the butter until light and fluffy, then whisk in the icing sugar gradually until the mixture is light and fluffy. Stir in the cooled melted chocolate and then the egg yolks, one at a time. Thoroughly wash the beaters. In a separate bowl, whisk the egg whites to fairly stiff peaks.

Using a large balloon whisk, fold one-third of the egg whites into the batter, then fold one-third of the flour. Repeat twice more, folding in one-third of the ingredients each time.

Grease and flour a 500-g loaf tin. Pour the mixture into the prepared tin and bake for 50–55 minutes, until the cake pulls away from the sides of the tin. At the end of cooking time, turn off the oven, open the door and leave the cake to cool in the oven for about 10 minutes. Then tip the cake out on a wire rack to cool completely.

Spread the warm jam over the top of the cake and while it is setting, make the glaze. Break the chocolate into small pieces and melt in a bowl over a pan of hot but not boiling water. Make sure the base of the bowl does not touch the water. Stir and when melted, remove from the heat. Stir in the butter. Pour the glaze evenly over the cake and set aside to firm up.

To cut the cake, heat the blade of a serrated knife under hot running water, and dry it well (this is to avoid the glaze cracking). Cut into thin slices.

Schlagrahm
PERFECT WHIPPED CREAM

MAKES 500 ML

250 ml whipping cream

1–1½ tbsp caster sugar

Splash of light rum or
Grand Marnier (optional)

Chill a mixing bowl and electric mixer beaters in the fridge
for at least an hour.

Pour the cream into the chilled bowl and whisk, gradually
adding the sugar while whisking all the time, until the
cream starts to thicken into soft peaks. Test for sweetness and
adjust accordingly.

NOTE

If the cream is being used as a filling, you can add rum or Grand
Marnier for additional flavour. Whipped cream is popular in
Viennese cuisine and used often, not least of all with a *Schwarzen
Kaffee*, an espresso coffee served after lunch.

Torten

TORTES

In an Austrian household, tortes are usually made for special occasions only: birthdays, engagements, anniversaries. In Tante Hertha's days, you would also serve a torte after a formal lunch. Another equally elegant invite would be a request to *komm zum Schwarzen*, the literal translation of which is 'to come for a black coffee', signifying the time after lunch, usually at 2 pm, where coffee, often accompanied by freshly whipped cream, and a beautifully presented torte, would be served. Lunch would have taken place in the dining room, but for coffee, society ladies would meet for light conversation in the sun-filled salon, as Hertha's generation would have called a formal drawing room.

The salons of Hertha and her contemporaries were filled with family portraits covering faded pale pink or yellow painted walls, Biedermeier furniture, perhaps a card table in the corner, and a formality long faded away, gone with the endless summers and a time where immediate and extended family were as close as best friends, eager to catch up on the latest news. As a young girl visiting aunts and cousins, I remember the austere but comforting salons, impeccable and never-changing, somehow peaceful and familiar in their constancy.

Altwiener Topfentorte

OLD-WORLD VIENNA CURD TORTE

MAKES 8–10 SLICES

Extra-fine breadcrumbs, for dusting the cake tin

120 g unsalted butter, plus extra for greasing

120 g icing sugar

4 large eggs, separated

120 g (20% fat) curd cheese, sieved

Grated zest of ½ lemon

Pinch of salt

1–½ tsp vanilla sugar (see page 136), plus extra for dusting

120 g blanched ground almonds

Preheat the oven to 180°C/350°F/gas 4. Grease a 23-cm round springform cake tin and lightly dust with the breadcrumbs.

In the bowl of an electric mixer, cream the butter until light and fluffy, and gradually add the icing sugar until well-blended. Add one egg yolk at a time, whisking in between each addition. Now stir in the sieved curd cheese, lemon zest, salt and vanilla sugar. Set aside. Thoroughly wash the beaters.

In a separate bowl, whisk the egg whites to stiff peaks. Then alternate folding the egg whites and the ground almonds into the curd cheese/butter mixture. Do this gently and quickly.

Pour the mixture into the cake tin and bake for 50–60 minutes – the cake will start to pull away from the sides of the tin when ready.

Remove from the oven and turn out onto a wire rack to cool. Once cooled, dust with vanilla-flavoured icing sugar and serve.

NOTE

There is nothing quite like Austrian *Topfen*, whose closest English counterpart is light curd cheese or quark. Made from milk with no extra additives or salt, *Topfen* adds a light, smooth flavour to tortes and cakes. If you are finding it hard to source in your local supermarket, most European delicatessens should have a suitable match.

Falsche Sachertorte

FAUX SACHERTORTE

MAKES 8–10 SLICES

FOR THE BATTER

150 g unsalted butter

150 g icing sugar

3 large egg yolks

150 g dark (70% cocoa) chocolate

100 g ground walnuts

50 g plain flour

5 large egg whites

FOR THE GANACHE

125 ml whipping cream

50 g unsalted butter

125 g dark (70% cocoa) chocolate, coarsely chopped

Preheat the oven to 160°C /325°F/gas 3. Grease and lightly flour a 23-cm round springform cake tin.

Start by making the batter. Break the chocolate into small pieces and place in a heatproof bowl. Melt the chocolate, either by heating in a microwave for 20–30 seconds or by placing the bowl over a pan of just simmering water. Make sure the bowl is not touching the water and monitor carefully. Alternatively you can melt the chocolate the way Hertha would have done (see Note on page 122). Stir the chocolate until smooth and set aside to cool.

In the bowl of an electric mixer, cream the butter until light and fluffy, and gradually add two-thirds of the icing sugar and beat until well blended. Add one egg yolk at a time, whisking between each addition. Then stir in the chocolate.

In a separate bowl, beat the egg whites to soft peaks using an electric mixer. Beat in the remaining one-third of icing sugar until the texture is light and glossy.

Sieve the flour into a bowl with the ground walnuts. Fold half into the butter/sugar mixture, then fold in half the egg whites. Repeat with the other halves.

Pour the mixture into the prepared cake tin and bake for 55–60 minutes. Then turn off the oven but leave the cake inside with the oven door open for another 10 minutes before removing. Turn the cake out onto a wire rack when partially cooled.

While the cake is baking, make the ganache. Place the cream, butter and chocolate in a small stainless steel saucepan and heat over a medium to low heat, stirring continuously until the chocolate has melted. Remove from heat and pour into the bowl of an electric mixer. Refrigerate for about 15 minutes. When the edges of the ganache begin to harden, take it out of the refrigerator and whisk with an electric mixer until light and fluffy.

When the cake has completely cooled, spread the ganache evenly over the top and sides. Refrigerate for at least 1 hour before serving.

Haselnußcrèmetorte

HAZELNUT CREAM TORTE

MAKES 6 SLICES

FOR THE BATTER

40 g fine breadcrumbs

30 g plain flour

5 large eggs, separated

160 g icing sugar

120 g toasted ground hazelnuts

FOR THE NUT CREAM FILLING

80 g shelled almonds

80 g granulated sugar

100 g unsalted butter

100 g icing sugar

1 large egg, beaten

1 tbsp dark rum

Preheat the oven to 190°C/375°F/gas 5. Grease and lightly flour a 20-cm round springform cake tin.

Start by making the batter. In a bowl, mix the breadcrumbs with the flour and set aside. In a separate bowl, whisk the egg yolks with 140 g of the icing sugar until light and fluffy. Wash the beaters thoroughly.

In a third separate bowl, beat the egg whites to stiff peaks, beating in the remaining icing sugar. Alternately fold the egg whites, ground hazelnuts, and flour/breadcrumbs into the sugar/egg yolk mixture.

Pour the mixture into the prepared cake tin and bake for 45–50 minutes. Remove from the oven and allow to cool in the tin. Once cooled, remove the cake from the tin.

To make the nut cream filling, start by toasting the almonds. Spread them on a baking sheet and toast for 10 minutes, or until fragrant. Remove from the oven and reduce the temperature to 150°C/300°F/gas 2.

When cooled, coarsely chop the toasted nuts. Melt the sugar in a heavy saucepan over medium-low heat, stirring all the while until it caramelizes.

Remove the pan from the heat immediately and stir in the nuts. Promptly spread onto a lightly oiled baking sheet to cool. Once cooled, break into chunks, then pound coarsely (or more finely, depending on personal preference) in a mortar. Reserve 4 tablespoons for the topping.

In the bowl of an electric mixer, beat the butter, icing sugar and egg until light and fluffy, then stir in the caramelised almonds and the rum.

Slice the cake in half and spread two-thirds of the filling between the two layers. Spread the remaining filling over the top and sides of the cake. Sprinkle the top with the reserved caramelised almonds.

Linzertorte

LINZER TORTE

MAKES 6–8 SLICES

140 g caster sugar

140 g plain flour

140 g ground roasted hazelnuts

1 tsp ground cinnamon

140 g cold unsalted butter, diced

Grated zest of 1 lemon

Juice of 1 lemon

3 large egg yolks

180 g redcurrant, raspberry or plum jam (redcurrant is the classic choice)

Preheat the oven to 180°C/350°F/gas 4. Grind the roasted hazelnuts with half the sugar in a food processor until powdery – be careful not to over process as you do not want the mixture to turn into a paste.

Add the rest of the dry ingredients to the food processor, along with the diced butter. Process until the mixture resembles coarse breadcrumbs. Add the lemon zest, followed by the lemon juice and egg yolks and process again to form a dough. Form the dough into a ball, wrap in cling film and refrigerate for 1 hour.

Remove the dough from the fridge and knead quickly. Take two-thirds of the dough and press it into a 23-cm round springform tin, using your knuckles to firm it down. Pull the dough 2 cm up the sides of the tin. Evenly spread the base (but not the sides) with the jam. Roll out the remaining dough to a thickness of 3 mm and cut it into enough 12-mm wide strips to cover the cake. Place the strips across the top of the jam, like a lattice, trimming the strips to fit. Gently press the strips down with your fingers.

Bake for 45–50 minutes. Remove the cake from oven but do not remove it from the tin until it has cooled completely or it will crumble.

NOTE

If you like, you can brush the lattice strips with one egg yolk mixed with 1 tbsp milk. This will give the torte a shiny gloss and golden colour. Make sure the glaze does not spill onto the jam!

Mohntorte Tante Fränzchen

AUNT FRÄNZCHEN'S POPPY-SEED TORTE

MAKES 6–8 SLICES

200 g unsalted butter,
at room temperature

200 g icing sugar

6 large eggs, separated,
at room temperature

150 g ground poppy seeds

50 g ground almonds

2 tbsp dark rum

2 tbsp plain flour, sieved

Pinch of salt

About 5 tbsp redcurrant jam,
warmed and cooled

1 tbsp poppy seeds, to
decorate

FOR THE GLAZE

2 tbsp lemon juice

2 tbsp rum

250 g icing sugar

1–2 tbsp boiling water

Preheat the oven to 160°C/325°F/gas 3. Grease and lightly flour a 23-cm round springform cake tin. Line the bottom with baking parchment.

In the bowl of an electric mixer, cream the butter until light and fluffy. Gradually add the icing sugar, whisking between each addition. Add one yolk at a time, beating well between each addition, until fully incorporated. Transfer the mixture to a large bowl and mix in the ground poppy seeds, ground almonds and rum.

In a separate bowl, whisk the egg whites to fairly stiff peaks. Using a balloon whisk, alternately fold the egg whites into the butter/sugar mixture, with the sieved flour and salt.

Pour the batter into the cake tin and bake for 55–60 minutes. The cake is ready when it starts to pull away from the sides of the cake tin. Remove from the oven and turn the cake onto a wire rack to cool. You can even leave it overnight and glaze the next day so that the cake sets and mellows.

To make the glaze, mix the lemon juice and rum into the icing sugar, and add just enough boiling water to form a spreadable glaze.

Slice the cake in half and spread half the jam between the two cake layers. Spread the remaining jam thinly over the top and sides of the cake. Once the redcurrant jam has dried, spread the top and sides of the cake with your choice of glaze (either the one made here or the chocolate or lemon glazes on page 194). Sprinkle with a handful of poppy seeds to decorate.

> NOTE
> If you can't purchase ground poppy seeds, you can pulse them in an electric coffee grinder.

Nusstorte mit Mochacrème

NUT TORTE WITH MOCHA CREAM FILLING

MAKES 6–8 SLICES

FOR THE BATTER

40 g fine breadcrumbs, plus extra for 'flouring'

30 g plain flour

5 large eggs, separated

160 g icing sugar

120 g ground walnuts

FOR THE COFFEE FILLING

150 g unsalted butter

120 g icing sugar

1 large egg yolk

60 ml cold strong black coffee or espresso

1 tbsp vanilla sugar (optional) (see page 136)

EGG WHITE GLAZE

250–300 g icing sugar

2 tsp egg white

CHOCOLATE GLAZE

100 g plain chocolate (50% cocoa)

50 g unsalted butter

Preheat the oven to 190°C/375°F/gas 5. Grease and dust a 23-cm round springform cake tin with breadcrumbs (or ground almonds if you prefer).

Start by making the batter. In a bowl, mix the breadcrumbs with the flour and set aside. In a separate bowl, whisk the egg yolks with 140 g of the icing sugar until light and fluffy. Wash the beaters thoroughly.

In a third separate bowl, beat the egg whites to soft peaks, beating in the remaining icing sugar. Alternately fold the egg whites, ground walnuts, and flour/breadcrumbs into the sugar/egg yolk mixture.

Pour the mixture into the cake tin and bake for 45–50 minutes. Remove from the oven and allow to cool in the tin, then turn out onto a wire rack. Glaze with either the chocolate glaze or the egg white glaze.

To make the filling, cream the butter until light. Add the icing sugar and continue beating until very light and fluffy, then beat in the egg yolk. Stir in the cold coffee along with the vanilla sugar.

Mix the egg white into the icing sugar so that you have a spreadable icing.

Break the chocolate into small pieces and place in a heatproof bowl. Melt, either by heating in a microwave for 20–30 seconds or by placing the bowl over a pan of just simmering water. Make sure the bowl is not touching the water and monitor carefully. Alternatively you can melt the chocolate the way Hertha would have (see Note on page 122). When melted add the butter and stir to blend.

Sacher-Gugelhupf

HOTEL SACHER GUGELHOPF

MAKES 8 SLICES

FOR THE BATTER

120 g unsalted butter

170 g icing sugar

4 large egg yolks

Grated zest of 1 lemon

3 tbsp milk

200 g plain flour

2 tsp baking powder

4 large egg whites

60 g sultanas, dusted with flour

Preheat the oven to 180°C/350°F/gas 4. Generously grease and lightly flour a 20-cm ring mould.

In the bowl of an electric mixer, cream the butter until light and fluffy, and gradually add the icing sugar until well-blended. Add one egg yolk at a time, whisking in between each addition. Now stir in the lemon zest, milk and 30 g of the flour.

In a separate bowl, sieve the remaining flour with the baking powder. In another bowl, beat the egg whites to stiff peaks.

Using a spatula, fold one third of the flour mixture into the whipped butter, egg and sugar mixture, followed by the egg whites. Repeat twice more. Finally and swiftly, fold in the dusted sultanas.

Pour the mixture into the prepared cake tin and bake for about 1 hour, until deep golden in colour. Then remove the cake from the oven and allow to cool in the tin for 10–15 minutes before turning onto a wire rack to cool. When the cake has cooled completely, ice it with chocolate glaze (see page 194).

Orangenbuttercrèmetorte
ORANGE BUTTERCREAM TORTE

MAKES 6–8 SLICES

FOR THE BATTER

6 large egg yolks

140 g icing sugar

4 large egg whites

140 g ground almonds

20 g fine breadcrumbs, soaked in the juice of 1 orange

FOR THE FILLING

1 tsp plain flour

4 tbsp fresh orange juice

2 tbsp rum

4 large egg yolks

100 g unsalted butter, at room temperature

100 g icing sugar

Preheat the oven to 190°C/375°F/gas 5. Grease and lightly flour a 23-cm round springform cake tin.

In the bowl of an electric mixer, lightly beat the egg yolks. Add the icing sugar and beat to a very light colour. Thoroughly wash the beaters.

In a separate bowl, beat the egg whites to stiff peaks and gently fold them into the egg yolk/sugar mixture, adding the ground almonds and moistened breadcrumbs alternately.

Pour the mixture into the cake tin and bake for 40–45 minutes. Remove from the oven and allow the cake to cool in the tin for 15 minutes before turning it out onto a wire rack to cool.

To make the filling, mix the flour with the orange juice and rum in a small saucepan off the heat. Turn the heat on low, and add the egg yolks, stirring constantly until thickened. Remove from heat and set aside to cool.

Meanwhile, in the bowl of an electric mixer, cream the butter until light and fluffy, and gradually beat in the icing sugar. Very gradually beat in the cooled egg mixture, until fully incorporated.

Slice the cake in half and spread the filling between the two cake layers. Cover with one of the glazes on page 194.

Schokotorte

CHOCOLATE TORTE

MAKES 6–8 SLICES

80 g dark (70% cocoa) chocolate

80 g ground almonds

2 tbsp fine breadcrumbs

Pinch of salt

80 g unsalted butter

80 g icing sugar

4 large eggs, separated

Whipped cream, to serve

For the ganache, see page 185

Preheat the oven to 180°C/350°F/gas 4. Grease and lightly flour a 23-cm round springform cake tin.

Break the chocolate into small pieces and place in a heatproof bowl. Melt the chocolate, either by heating in a microwave for 20–30 seconds or by placing the bowl over a pan of just simmering water. Make sure the bowl is not touching the water and monitor carefully. Alternatively you can melt the chocolate the way Hertha would have done (see Note on page 122). Stir the chocolate until smooth and set aside to cool.

In a bowl, mix the ground almonds, breadcrumbs and salt and set aside. In a separate bowl, cream the butter until light. Add the icing sugar, one tablespoon at a time, beating between each addition, until the mixture is light and fluffy. Then stir in the cooled chocolate.

In a separate bowl, whisk the egg whites to stiff peaks and gently fold into the creamed butter mixture one third at a time, alternating with the ground almond mixture, until all has been incorporated.

Pour the mixture into the prepared cake tin and bake for about 50 minutes. To test the cake, insert a toothpick into its centre. If it comes out clean and the cake pulls away from the sides of the pan, it is ready. Turn off the heat but leave the cake in the oven with the door open for 10 minutes. Remove the cake from the oven and when it has cooled more, turn it out onto a wire rack to cool.

Slice the cake in half and spread half the ganache between the two cake layers. Spread the remaining ganache over the top and sides of the cake. For a fancy effect, sprinkle chopped pistachios on top. Cut into generous slices and serve with whipped cream.

Topfentorte Lene

LENE'S CHEESE CURD TORTE

MAKES 8 SLICES

250 g plain flour

1 tsp baking powder

1 large egg yolk

3–4 tbsp soured cream

120 g icing sugar

60 g unsalted butter, cold

FOR THE FILLING

1 tbsp plain flour

2 tbsp cornflour

1 tsp baking powder

200 ml soured cream

2 large egg yolks

Juice and zest of ½ lemon

380 g curd cheese (20% fat)

4 tbsp granulated sugar

80 g sultanas

3 large egg whites

Grease and lightly flour a 23-cm round springform cake tin.

Sieve the flour with the baking powder on a clean work surface. Thinly slice the cold butter into the flour and pinch the mixture between your fingertips until it resembles coarse crumbs.

Mix in the sugar, then make a well in the centre. In a bowl, mix the egg yolk with the soured cream and pour into the centre. Knead into a dough using the heels of your hands for 2–3 minutes. The dough should be smooth and not stick to the work surface. Shape the dough into a ball, wrap it in cling film and refrigerate for 1 hour.

Remove the dough from the fridge and roll it out to a circle that is 5 cm larger than the base of your cake tin. Transfer to the tin and gently press it onto the base and sides of the pan. Chill for 15 minutes while preparing the filling. Preheat the oven to 180°C/350°F/gas 4.

To make the filling, mix the flour with the cornflour and baking powder and set aside. Press the curd cheese through a sieve into a large bowl. Add the sugar, lemon juice and zest, soured cream, egg yolks, mixing it all together with a wooden spoon. Then sieve the flour mixture over the mixture in the bowl. Finally, add the sultanas and fold them in with the rest.

Beat the egg whites until soft peaks form. Using a spatula, gently fold the egg whites into the cheese mixture. Empty the filling into the prepared tin and bake for 10 minutes, then reduce the heat to 160°C/325°F/gas 3 and bake for another 45 minutes, until golden and the cake begins to pull away from the sides of the tin. Turn off the heat, open the oven door, and leave the cake inside for 10 minutes.

Place the cake on a cooling rack and cool for 10 minutes, before removing the sides of the tin.

Tante Herthas Geburtstagstorte

TANTE HERTHA'S BIRTHDAY TORTE

SERVES 6

FOR THE BATTER

200 g dark (70% cocoa) chocolate

200 g unsalted butter, at room temperature

200 g icing sugar

4 large eggs, separated

50 g plain flour

FOR THE PRALINE

100 g granulated sugar

100 g hazelnuts, toasted

TOASTING HAZELNUTS

Preheat the oven to 180°C/350°F/gas 4. Spread the nuts on a baking sheet and toast for 10 minutes, or until fragrant. Remove from the oven.

Preheat the oven to 160°C/325°F/gas 3. Grease and lightly flour a 20-cm round springform cake tin.

Break the chocolate into small pieces and place in a heatproof bowl. Melt the chocolate, either by heating in a microwave for 20–30 seconds or by placing the bowl over a pan of just simmering water. Make sure the bowl is not touching the water and monitor carefully. Alternatively you can melt the chocolate the way Hertha would have done (see Note on page 122). Stir the chocolate until smooth and set aside to cool.

In the bowl of an electric mixer, cream the butter until light and fluffy, and gradually add the icing sugar, increasing the speed for 1–2 minutes. Add one egg yolk at a time, whisking in between each addition. Now stir in the melted chocolate until well blended.

In a separate bowl, beat the egg whites to stiff peaks. Using a spatula, fold the egg whites into the butter/chocolate mixture.

Divide the mixture into two portions, with one portion slightly larger than the other. Set aside the larger portion in a cool place (but not in the refrigerator as it needs to be spreadable). Stir the flour into the smaller portion and pour this into the prepared cake tin.

Bake for 20 minutes, then remove from oven and turn out onto a wire rack to cool. Spread the mixture that had been set aside on the top of the cake.

To make the praline, (this can be made in advance), coarsely chop the toasted hazelnuts. Melt the sugar in a medium saucepan, stirring all the while, until it caramelises. Remove from the heat and stir in the hazelnuts. Immediately spread onto a lightly oiled baking sheet to cool. Once cooled, break into chunks, then pound coarsely (or more finely, depending on personal preference) in a mortar.

Sprinkle the praline on top of the cake. Refrigerate for several hours before serving.

Crèmes und Marmeladen

PUDDINGS AND JAMS

In the early 1950s some time after the war, Tante Hertha began a small catering business, her reputation as a fine cook preceding her among a large circle of friends and family. Her signature creations were her heavenly jams and marmalades. Orders were placed every year and Hertha, at this time living with a cousin and an aunt, singlehandedly began the process of jam-making in season. My mother can remember the waft of oranges lingering throughout the beautiful flat during Vienna's icy cold winter months when bitter oranges from Seville became available. In mid to late summer, Hertha would purchase freshly plucked apricots, plums, strawberries and raspberries from the Naschmarkt for her summer jams. An annual holiday was always scheduled for late August when the final glasses of jams had been sealed and stored under beds, on top of armoires, in corners of the kitchen, the pantry, the salon. The coveted jams and marmalades were collected upon Hertha's return; Hertha refreshed from her holidays, her clients happy, and her cousin Christl relieved by the return of a slightly more spacious flat for another six months.

Dali-Crème

VANILLA MOUSSE WITH A RASPBERRY OR STRAWBERRY COULIS

SERVES 4

FOR THE MOUSSE

175 ml whipping cream

80 g caster sugar

¼ tsp vanilla extract

4 large egg yolks

1½ tbsp / 10 g gelatine powder

2 tbsp lemon juice

Grated zest of ½ lemon

FOR THE COULIS

250 g fresh or frozen raspberries, defrosted

1–2 tbsp Framboise or Kirsch (optional)

80 g icing sugar, or to taste

Start by making the mousse. Whisk the whipping cream with ½ tablespoon of the sugar and vanilla extract until it starts to thicken and form soft peaks. Refrigerate until ready to use.

In the bowl of an electric mixer, combine the egg yolks and gradually beat in the remaining sugar. Set the bowl over a pan of simmering water, making sure the base of the bowl does not touch the water, and whisk with a balloon whisk for 5–8 minutes, until the mixture is thick. Remove from the heat and whisk on medium speed for 5 minutes.

Measure 125 ml cold water into a heat-resistant bowl and sprinkle the gelatine into it to soften. Then place the bowl over a pan of simmering water to melt, while stirring all the time.

Gradually pour the melted gelatine into the egg and sugar mixture and whisk on a low speed. Whisk in the lemon juice and the grated zest until incorporated.

Set the mixture over ice, stirring regularly until it begins to set, then immediately remove from the ice and gently fold in the whipped cream with a balloon whisk or spatula. Pour into a rinsed 1-litre jelly mould, cover and chill for at least 6 hours. Keeps for up to two days in the fridge.

To make the coulis, purée the raspberries in a blender with the alcohol of your choice. Strain through a fine sieve, using the underside of a spoon to push through the fruit. Stir in the icing sugar and pour into a small jug, ready to serve. Refrigerate before serving.

Eiercognac Tante Putzi

AUNT PUTZI'S EGG COGNAC

MAKES 1½ LITRES

750 ml full-fat milk

260 g icing sugar

30 g vanilla sugar
(see page 136)

5 large egg yolks

250 ml vodka

Rinse a medium-size saucepan in water (but do not dry). Pour in the milk, along with 100 g of the icing sugar and the vanilla sugar. Slowly bring to the boil, then reduce the heat and simmer for 30 minutes, uncovered. Remove from the heat and set aside to cool. Then strain the milk through a sieve into a large jug or bowl to leave the skin behind.

In the bowl of an electric mixer, whisk the egg yolks with the remaining icing sugar (160 g) until pale. Ladle a quarter of the strained milk into the mixture, and whisk on the lowest setting. Now add the remaining milk and the vodka and whisk very briefly to incorporate.

Transfer to a sterilised bottle and refrigerate for four to five days before sampling this delicious tipple. Keeps well, refrigerated, for up to four months.

Marillen/fruchtkompott

APRICOT/OTHER FRUIT COMPOTE

SERVES 6

1 kg ripe apricots

300 g granulated sugar

Wash and stone the apricots, then cut them in half. Place them in a bowl and pour the sugar over them. Cover with a lid and let them stand at room temperature overnight.

The next day, transfer the apricots and sugar to a pan and cook over a low heat to start off with, then increase the heat gradually until the fruit comes to a boil. Reduce the heat and simmer for 20–25 minutes. Turn off the heat then set aside to cool.

This compote is delicious served with a dollop of crème fraîche and for an extra flavourful touch, sprinkled with chopped pistachios or coarsely chopped roasted walnuts. Compotes also accompany many pancake-style dishes such as Kaiserschmarren (see page 148) or Palatschinken (see page 149).

Orangenschaum

ORANGE FOAM JELLY

MAKES 500 ML

350 g caster sugar

25 g gelatine powder

Zest of 1 lemon

Juice of 3 oranges (300 ml)

Juice of 2 small lemons (150 ml)

Pour 75 ml of water in a pan and tip in the sugar. Place on a low heat until the sugar has dissolved, stirring occasionally. Remove from the heat.

Pour 115 ml hot but not boiling in a heat-resistant bowl and sprinkle the gelatine into it, stirring with a fork until dissolved. Add this to the hot sugar water, stirring vigorously to incorporate the gelatine into the sugar water. Stir in the lemon zest and set aside to cool.

Strain the orange and lemon juices through a sieve, then whisk the juice into the cooled gelatine mixture using an electric mixer. Whisk on high speed for several minutes until the liquid turns light and foamy. Pour into a 500-ml mould or plastic container and refrigerate for several hours or overnight.

Schokoladencrème

SOFT CHOCOLATE PUDDING

SERVES 8

Butter, for greasing

Icing sugar or cocoa powder,
for dusting

150 g plain (50% cocoa)
chocolate

375 ml whipping cream

6 large egg yolks

6 tbsp granulated sugar

Prepare eight 5-cm deep 7.5-cm round ramekins. Lightly grease and dust with icing sugar or cocoa powder.

Break the chocolate into small pieces in an ovenproof bowl and place in the centre of a preheated 100°C /200°F/gas ¼ oven until it has just melted to a silky smooth texture, about 10–15 minutes. Remove from oven, stir until smooth and set aside to cool. Increase the oven temperature to 160°C/325°F/gas 3.

In a stainless steel saucepan on a very low heat, slowly bring the cream just to the brink of boiling point. Pour in the melted chocolate, stir and set aside to cool.

Using an electric mixer, whisk the egg yolks with the sugar, starting on a low speed and gradually increasing to medium and then high, until thick, creamy and pale. In a slow stream, add the cream/chocolate mixture, whisking at the lowest speed.

Divide the mixture equally into the ramekins and place them in a roasting tin. Carefully pour boiling water into the tin (not into the ramekins!) until the water is 1.5 cm up the sides of the ramekins. Bake for 35–40 minutes, or until risen and the tops feel firm to the touch.

Topfencrème

QUARK CRÈME

SERVES 4

250 ml quark

250 ml soured cream

250 ml plain yoghurt

3 tbsp light brown sugar

2 tsp lemon juice, or to taste

In a mixing bowl, whisk the quark with an electric mixer, then whisk in the soured cream, yoghurt, sugar and lemon juice, to taste. The consistency should be that of a thick cream.

This is a delicious light crème, served either on its own or with seasonal berries. It can also be poured over vanilla ice cream. If you make a mistake and it turns out too runny, this is not a problem – refrigerate and have it as a yoghurt-type drink instead.

Schokoladenreis

CHOCOLATE RICE PUDDING

SERVES 6–8

200 g short-grain rice or Italian arborio rice

750 ml milk

70 g unsalted butter

70 g granulated sugar

3–4 large eggs, separated

80 g dark (70% cocoa) chocolate, grated

Icing sugar, for sprinkling (optional)

Preheat the oven to 180°C/350°F/gas 4. Generously grease a 22-cm round soufflé dish.

Rinse the rice under hot running water. Pour the milk in a pan and cook the rice in the milk until al dente. Set aside to cool.

In the bowl of an electric mixer, cream the butter with the sugar until light and fluffy. Add the egg yolks, one at the time, whisking between each addition. Thoroughly wash the beaters, then in a separate bowl, whisk the egg whites to stiff peaks.

Stir the cooled rice into the creamed butter mixture and fold in the beaten egg whites. Place half the mixture into the prepared soufflé dish. Sprinkle over the grated chocolate and cover with the rest of the rice mixture. Sprinkle the top with sugar, if desired. Bake for 40 minutes, or until top is light golden. For complete decadence, serve with a dollop of whipped cream.

Jams

There are a few basic rules for successful jam-making:

❋ Use impeccably clean, stainless steel equipment and pots, ensuring there are no food odours.

❋ The jars in which you store the jam must be made of glass, sterilized and filled with jam while the jam is still hot.

❋ To sterilize the jars and lids, wash them in hot soapy water, then rinse thoroughly with hot water. Place clean jars lying down in a large pan, cover completely with cold water, cover pan, bring to boil and continue boiling, covered for 20 minutes. Then with tongs and rubber gloves, remove them from the pan, tip out the water and drain. Stand upright on a clean towel to air dry.

❋ To sterilize the jars in a dishwasher, use the rinse cycle at the hottest temperature, and do not use dishwashing powder.

❋ Use a silver spoon (without superstition!) for testing whether the jam has reached 'setting point'. To do this, drop a teaspoon of the mixture onto a cold saucer, which had been chilled in the freezer for a few minutes, then return it to the freezer for 5 minutes, until the jam has cooled to room temperature. If it is ready, a skin will have formed on the surface of the jam and it will wrinkle when you push it with your finger.

❋ The fruit should be as freshly picked as possible and slightly under-ripe as this is the stage at which the pectin content is at its highest.

❋ Filled jars are best stored in a cool, dry, dark place for up to one year. Once opened, refrigerate and keep for up to six months.

Marillenmarmelade

APRICOT JAM

MAKES 3–4 250-ML JARS

1 kg ripe apricots (stoned weight)

500 g granulated sugar

Wash the apricots, halve them and remove the stones and any blemishes, then weigh them. Cut the fruit into small pieces.

Put the fruit in a stainless steel saucepan and bring gently to a boil. Simmer, uncovered, until the fruit is soft, about 15 minutes. Stir frequently.

Add the sugar to the pan, increasing the heat to high, stirring so that the sugar dissolves quickly (the sugar must dissolve before mixture comes to a boil).

After this point, bring the jam to a quick boil, stirring regularly to prevent the jam sticking to the base of the pan, particularly towards the end of cooking time. The mixture should be thick and ready to set. This will take approximately 30–40 minutes.

Check the setting point of the jam (see page 214 for setting point). Then remove from heat and immediately transfer into hot, sterilized jars (see page 214). Wipe the rims clean and seal once the jam is cold.

Himbeermarmelade

RASPBERRY JAM

MAKES 2–3 250-ML JARS

500 g jam sugar

500 g raspberries, fresh
or frozen

1 tbsp lemon juice

OR TRY THIS…

Instead of just
raspberries, use a mix of
250 g raspberries and
250 g redcurrants. In
this case, both fruits will
have to be harvested
during their growing
season. For this version,
the lemon juice will be
omitted but the sugar
quantity stays the same.

Preheat the oven to 150°C/300°F/gas 2.

Warm the sugar in the oven in a heat-resistant bowl for
8–10 minutes.

In a large, shallow stainless steel saucepan, combine the fruit
and the lemon juice, and simmer gently for 5 minutes, stirring it
once or twice. Tip in the warmed sugar all in one go. Stir to dissolve
the sugar, then increase the heat and bring to the boil.

Boil uncovered, without stirring, for about 12 minutes, until the
jam sets when tested (see page 214 for setting point). Remove from
heat and immediately transfer to hot, sterilized jars (see page 214).
Wipe the rims clean and seal once the jam is cold.

Orangenmarmelade

ORANGE MARMALADE

MAKES 12 250-ML JARS

1 kg Seville oranges

2 litres water

2 kg granulated sugar

Wash the oranges (as you will be using the peel). Cut them into quarters and shred them very finely, using a mandolin or the thinnest slicer on a food processor (do not peel the oranges). Reserve the pips: keep them in a bowl and cover them with 250 ml of the water. Cover with cling film and let stand overnight.

Put the shredded oranges in a large bowl, pour over the remaining water, cover with cling film and let stand overnight.

The following day, wrap the pips in a piece of muslin and secure with a knot. Pour the water in which the pips have been standing into the bowl with the shredded oranges.

Transfer the shredded oranges and their juice into a large stainless steel pan. Drop the muslin bag in the pan. Bring to the boil, then lower the heat and simmer, covered, for about 30–40 minutes, until the fruit is medium-soft, then discard the muslin bag and its contents.

While still on a low heat, add the sugar, stirring until it has dissolved. Then bring to the boil again, uncovered, without stirring, for about 30 minutes, or until the marmalade reaches setting point (see page 214). Then remove the pan from the heat. Pour into hot, sterilized jars (see page 214) using a ladle. Wipe the rims clean and seal once the jam is cold.

Powidel

PLUM PRESERVE

MAKES 500 ML

300 g pitted prunes

2 tsp grated zest of an orange or lemon

80 g homemade (see page 216) or shop-bought raspberry jam

2 tsp lemon juice

In a pan, bring the prunes with 175 ml water and the orange/lemon zest to a boil, then reduce the heat and simmer for 20 minutes.

Remove from the heat and when cooled, pulse in a food processor until smooth. Transfer to a bowl and stir in the raspberry jam with the lemon juice.

Store in a glass jar with a tight-fitting lid. Refrigerate and allow the flavours to 'mellow' for a few days before sampling. Once opened, the plum preserve will keep for several weeks when refrigerated.

This is a modern method; the traditional recipe would have taken almost a week to prepare!

Index

Acknowledgements

To our friends at New Holland, with a very special thank you to Steve Connolly for his effusive *jawohl!* to the concept, to the Rights ladies and to our publisher, the calm and collected Clare Sayer. Also to the wonderful team of creative collaborators: Jacqui Caulton, a true artist and brilliant designer; Tara Fisher; Roisin Nield; Annie Rigg; and our copy editor, my lovely and highly exacting friend Corinne Masciocchi.

To:
Alexandra Koken, the Audrey Hepburn look-alike who first translated the worn pages of Tante Hertha's collection into English; the artists Barbara and Zafer Baran for so delicately handling these nearly century-old pages into legible working copies, and to Peter Mikl and Waltraud Strummer of the Austrian Cultural Forum for graciously hosting us to celebrate the cookbook's debut. To Michel Moushabeck of Interlink Publishing, close colleague and friend and now, with much joy, our US publisher.

Sarah al-Hamad, a dear friend and inspiration for the book. Without Sarah and her own historical cookbook, we would not have had the self-belief to go forward. To her partner Matthew Bishop, another *Feinschmecker* who approved of the testing with gusto. Photographer and friend Jon Meade on his hotshot assignment to Vienna, managing to encapsulate the essence of the city in just one day with over 200 incredible shots (and a few Demel chocolate boxes to spare). And to our very special muse, Michelle Lo.

The many Londoners, New Yorkers and Torontonians full of enthusiasm and encouragement (and eagerly, patiently awaiting further recipe sampling). Among them: David Cormack; Jeannine and Harrison Dillon; Gary Holmes; Lisa Honig for our imaginative cover and title pitches; Marla Hurov; Petra Kwan; Kristin Lauhn-Jensen; Sandy Levine; Joanne Shurvell; Eva Svec; Mindy Tenenbaum; Sandra Worden and Lori Zajkowski; and with eternal gratitude to Lisa Hostein, who for over twenty-five years, from London, Ontario to London, England, has so tirelessly reiterated: 'Just get in there and write!'

Anne Bieker; Elisabeth Gulacsy; Helga Hödl; Tatjana Panceva; Anna and Sharon Schauenstein, Vlasta Svec and the dashing Chris Oldfield for their priceless recipe homages. To the original girls from Graz: Kerstin Bieker, Franscesca Bubna-Kasteliz, Judith Scholes.

Most importantly, to our family, distanced only by the geography of fate. To the Austrians and *Ausgewanderten*, most notably Georg von Baich for his first intrepid photo shoot to a somewhat rainy Vienna and Graz, handled like a pro; Paul and Marie von Baich, and Theodor and Ina Baich for their enchanting heartfelt recollections of Tante Hertha; and to the beloved Tante Li Bubna. To cousins Barbara and her husband Philip Manby; and Andrew Lowe, the most unique and generous man gracing our English/Scottish family tree. To Bernard and Bryan, always.

Himbeersaft

Auf 3 l. zerdrückte Himbeeren 2 l. Wasser u. 4 Dk. zu
Weinsteinsäure lässt das Ganze 48 Stunden stehen, seih
es durch ein Tuch, durchdrücken. Man lässt den
Saft 48 Stunden stehen (noch einmal) da er sich
setzen muß, u. gibt auf 1/2 l. Saft 56 Dk. Zucker
lässt das Ganze an einen kühlen Ort stehen. Ist der
Zucker aufgelöst, füllt man den Saft in Flaschen
u. verbindet sie mit Draganten u. weißen Stoff

Orangenmarmelade

Auf 1 Kg. Orangen 1 Kg. Zucker. Feine Orangen werden
abgewaschen, dann sehr dünn abgeschält, die weiße
Haut ganz abgezogen u. entfernt. Die Schalen werden
sehr fein nudlig geschnitten, dann gießt man auf 1 Kg.
Orangen samt der Schale 2 l. Wasser u. lässt das Ganze
über Nacht stehen. Den nächsten Tag werden die Orangen
ohne Zucker 2 Stunden gekocht. Die Hälfte der Kerne
werden in Dragantinsäckchen getan u. mit gekocht
Hierauf kommt der Zucker hinein u. 1/2 Stunde
unter rühren kochen. Heiß in Gläser füllen. Man
gibt von den Schalen bei 2 Kg. Orangen, 10 Dk. weg.
Die weiße Haut abkriegen, u. um dieses Gewicht mehr
Zucker geben. Die abgeschälten Orangen werden in
Scheiben geschnitten, dabei die Kerne herausgenommen